3-

I
WISH
I'D SAID
THAT!

I WISH I'D SAID THAT!

ILLUSTRATED BY
HEATH

WRITTEN BY
NICK HARRIS

CASTLE

First published in 1984.
This edition published in 1988 by
arrangement with Octopus Books Limited.

CASTLE
A Division of
BOOK SALES, INC.
110 Enterprise Avenue
Secaucus, NJ   07094

ISBN 1-55521-163-1

Printed and bound in the United Kingdom by
William Clowes Ltd, Beccles

CONTENTS

INSTANT QUIPS

A collection of witty epigrams and wisecracks.

There is nothing more satisfying than a witty riposte. Unfortunately, most of us think of the perfect response only hours later – usually in the bath! The following collection of verbal gems was spoken or written by people whose instant wit is a constant source of envy – and delight!

With A Twist

Be warned! You are about to read some distinctly warped pieces of wisdom which make hay with familiar phrases and ideas

Essayist **Charles Lamb**:

> *'The greatest pleasure I know is to do good by stealth, and to have it found out by accident.'*

Jerome K. Jerome, author of *Three Men in a Boat*, argued that

> *'It is always the best policy to speak the truth, unless of course you are an exceptionally good liar.'*

According to **Sir Winston Churchill**:

> *'Men occasionally stumble over the truth, but most of them pick themselves up and hurry off as if nothing had happened.'*

The American satirist **Mark Twain** was responsible for the following highly moral reflections:

'To be good is noble, but to teach others to be good is nobler — and less trouble.'

'The holy passion of Friendship is of so sweet and steady and loyal and enduring a nature that it will last through a whole lifetime, if not asked to lend money.'

'Always do right: this will gratify some people and astonish the rest.'

The wily French statesman Talleyrand, mastermind behind the favourable peace terms of the Congress of Vienna in 1815, was — perhaps understandably — a confirmed cynic:

'Mistrust first impulses, they are always good.'

When Shakespeare wrote the immortal 'Brevity is the soul of wit' he couldn't know that **Dorothy Parker** would cap it with:

'Brevity is the soul of lingerie.' *BOOM!*

BOOM!

Austrian novelist **Robert Musil** on the modern world and its problems:

'Progress would be wonderful — if only it would stop.'

Damon Runyon adapted the Bible to the outlook of gambling guys and dolls, advising:

> *'The race is not always to the swift, nor the battle to the strong, but that's the way to bet.'*

Worldly wisdom from American humorist **Artemus Ward**:

> *'Thrice is he armed that hath his quarrel just – and four times he who gets his fist in fust.'*

Crackerbarrel philosophy from **Edward Noyes Westcott**:

> *'Do unto the other feller the way he'd like to do unto you, an' do it fust.'*

Immoral moral reflections were a speciality of Irish playwright **George Bernard Shaw**:

> *'Do not do unto others as you would they should do unto you. Their tastes may not be the same.'*

> *'The British churchgoer prefers a severe preacher because he thinks a few home truths will do his neighbours no harm.'*

> *'Martyrdom . . . is the only way in which a man can become famous without ability.'*

Heinrich Heine, German poet:

> *'One should forgive one's enemies, but not before they are hanged.'*

Lord Melbourne, British prime minister and friend of Queen Victoria, was religious — when he was in a church. Shocked by a sermon, he once remarked:

> *'Things have come to a pretty pass when religion is allowed to invade the sphere of private life.'*

Will Rogers, American humorist:

> *'Everything is funny as long as it is happening to somebody else.'*

NICE ONE

C. E. Montague, a journalist, served at the front in the First World War but found that there was more hysteria *behind* the lines. He wrote:

> *'War hath no fury like a non-combatant.'*

American novelist **James Branch Cabell**:

> *'The optimist proclaims that we live in the best of all possible worlds, and the pessimist fears this is true.'*

Arthur Bloch, shrewd commentator on contemporary society, calls this Jones's Law:

'The man who can smile when things go wrong has thought of someone he can blame it on.'

The American poet **Robert Frost** showed perfect understanding of the psychology of work:

'The brain is a wonderful organ. It starts working the moment you get up in the morning and does not stop until you get into the office.'

Poul Anderson, writer of science fiction, expressed his confidence in the power of the human mind, writing:

'I have yet to see any problem, however complicated, which, when looked at in the right way, did not become more complicated.'

G. K. Chesterton, English master of paradox, noted the social revolution that occurred when the invention of the typewriter created new job opportunities for women:

'Twenty million young women rose to their feet with the cry "We will not be dictated to," and promptly became stenographers.'

The American scientist **Paul Ehrlich** on technology, ancient and modern:

'To err is human but to really foul things up requires a computer.'

The film comedian **W. C. Fields**, bumbling and bad-tempered, came up with this inspiring thought:

'If at first you don't succeed, try, try again. Then give up. No use being a damn fool about it.'

13

Old-fashioned morality – according to **Robert Benchley**:

'A dog teaches a boy fidelity, perseverance, and to turn around three times before lying down.'

Oscar Wilde on how to secure a stable relationship:

'To love oneself is the beginning of a lifelong romance.'

Benjamin Franklin, American revolutionary leader and writer, identified one of the drawbacks of self-love:

'He that falls in love with himself will have no rivals.'

Film actress **Lily Tomlin** on the human condition:

'We're all in this together – by ourselves.'

A profoundly self-critical thought from film star **Ava Gardner**:

'Deep down, I'm pretty superficial.'

The flamboyant Irish dramatist **Oscar Wilde** made his own publicity. He believed that

'There is only one thing in the world worse than being talked about, and that is not being talked about.'

American art historian **Bernard Berenson**:

> *'Consistency requires you to be as ignorant today as you were a year ago.'*

Labour firebrand **Aneurin Bevan** had little time for compromise:

> *'We know what happens to people who stay in the middle of the road. They get run over.'*

BOOM!
BOOM!

The American comedienne **Phyllis Diller** has this advice to give on the subject of domestic relations:

> *'Never go to bed mad. Stay up and fight.'*

Sir James Barrie was the author of *Peter Pan*, the sentimental story of a boy who refused to grow up. But Barrie could still be irritated by his juniors, snapping:

> *'I am not young enough to know everything.'*

Oscar Wilde noted the freedom enjoyed by children in the United States:

> *'In America, the young are always ready to give to those who are older than themselves the benefit of their inexperience.'*

The Duke of Windsor (ex-King Edward VIII) put it another way:

'The thing that impresses me most about America is the way parents obey their children.'

Hollywood star **John Barrymore** didn't believe that virtue was its own reward. In fact —

'The good die young — because they see it's no use living if you've got to be good.'

Bernard Shaw:

'Youth is a wonderful thing; what a crime to waste it on children.'

Oscar Wilde doubted whether age brought wisdom, saying of an acquaintance:

'He is old enough to know worse.'

American essayist **Logan Pearsall Smith**:

'There is more felicity on the far side of baldness than young men can possibly imagine.'

William Feather, American author:

> *'Setting a good example for your children takes all the fun out of middle age.'*

American humorist **Kin Hubbard** thought being 'grown up' and good was a delusion:

> *'Boys will be boys, and so will a lot of middle-aged men.'*

French film star **Maurice Chevalier**:

> *'Old age isn't so bad when you consider the alternative.'*

Of one of his characters, American novelist **Joseph Heller** writes:

> *'He had decided to live forever, or die in the attempt.'*

GROAN!

In the French film *Breathless*, a smooth and successful writer is asked whether he has any ambition still to be fulfilled. Indeed he does:

> *'To become immortal, and then to die.'*

American comedian **Woody Allen**:

> *'It's not that I'm afraid to die. I just don't want to be there when it happens.'*

Summing up the meaning of human existence, writer-performer **Quentin Crisp** says:

> *'Life was a funny thing that happened to me on the way to the grave.'*

Money Matters

The possession or acquisition of wealth has yielded a glittering crop of wisecracks and ironic remarks over the years, as the following examples bear witness:

Conversation recorded by the novelist **Scott Fitzgerald**, who was dazzled by the glamour of the rich:

FITZGERALD: *The rich are different from us.*
ERNEST HEMINGWAY: *Yes, they have more money.*

The American critic **John Leonard** made the same point with more sophistication:

'The rich are different from you and me because they have more credit.'

'Red Hot Momma' blues singer **Sophie Tucker** summed up her own experience:

'I have been poor and I have been rich. Rich is better.'

The rich, although more fortunate than many, may yet behave decently. One of the dukes of **Argyll** remarked:

> *'As far as I'm concerned there are only two kinds of people in the world. Those who are nice to their servants and those who aren't.'*

How rich is rich? According to multi-millionaire **John Jacob Astor III**:

> *'A man who has a million dollars is as well off as if he were rich.'*

Wealth is a shield against even the harshest criticisms, as the glittering showman **Liberace** pointed out:

> *'What you said hurt me very much. I cried all the way to the bank.'*

— *TAKE THAT!* —

American journalist **Earl Wilson**:

> *'Success is just a matter of luck. Ask any failure.'*

American comedian **Jack Benny**, famed for his supposed meanness, is said to have been held up one day by a gangster.

GANGSTER: *Your money or your life!*

Pause.

BENNY: *I'm thinking it over.*

In the bad old days, when the husband controlled all the money in a family, there were many male fortune hunters. The novelist **Henry Fielding** described one scoundrel like this:

> *'His designs were strictly honourable, as the saying is; that is, to rob a lady of her fortune by way of marriage.'*

Girls too can be shrewd when it comes to romance – like Anita Loos's blonde heroine **Lorelei Lee** in *Gentlemen Prefer Blondes*:

> *'Kissing your hand may make you feel very good, but a diamond bracelet lasts for ever.'*

Dorothy Parker bemoaned her failure as a gold-digger:

> *Why is it no one ever sent me yet*
> *One perfect limousine, do you suppose?*
> *Ah no, it's always just my luck to get*
> *One perfect rose.*

Much loved and often married, Hollywood star **Zsa Zsa Gabor** remembered that:

> *'I never hated a man enough to give him his diamonds back.'*

One of the United States' Founding Fathers, **Benjamin Franklin**, handed out much solid practical advice, including this:

'If you would know the value of money, go and try to borrow some.'

Film star **Lana Turner** describes the perfect marriage:

'A successful man is one who makes more money than his wife can spend. A successful woman is one who can find such a man.'

In the movie *The Producers*, **Bialystok (Zero Mostel)** urges Leo (Gene Wilder) to seize his (crooked) opportunity while he can:

> *'Leo, he who hesitates is poor!'*

Quentin Crisp's view of social mobility:

> *'Never keep up with the Joneses. Drag them down to your level. It's cheaper.'*

The famous 18th century playwright **Sheridan** was never out of debt, but still managed to take a fine town house and furnish it. He told a friend that everything was 'going like clockwork'.
'Yes, I know what you mean,' answered the friend:

> *'Tick! Tick! Tick!'*

When pressed for payment by one of his many creditors, **Sheridan** said:

> *'You know it is not in my interest to pay the principal; nor is it my principle to pay the interest.'*

Sheridan was an Irishman. When asked why his name did not begin with 'O', the ever-penurious playwright answered:

> *'No family has a better right to an O than our family, for in truth we owe everybody.'*

SHOW STOPPERS

The larger-than-life figures of the entertainment business have been known to inspire and produce off-the-cuff lines which would make any scriptwriter green with envy:

The great showman **Phineas T. Barnum** knew that there were fortunes to be made in show business, since

> *'Every crowd has a silver lining.'*

Columbia executive **Harry Cohn** hints at how Hollywood got its results in this description of a budding actress of the silver screen:

> *'She's got talent and personality. Give me two years and I'll make her an overnight star.'*

Hollywood producer **Sam Goldwyn** was famous for making gaffes in his own brand of mangled English. But some of his remarks were shrewder than they seemed:

> *'Anyone who goes to a psychiatrist should have his head examined.'*

> *'What we want is a story that starts with an earthquake and works its way up to a climax.'*

Pianist and mordant wit **Oscar Levant**:

> *'Strip away the phoney tinsel of Hollywood and you find the real tinsel underneath.'*

In the 1930s **Mae West** played the bad girl who gloried in a lurid past – and present – as the following remarks demonstrate:

> *'I used to be Snow White, but I drifted.'*

> GIRL: *Goodness, what beautiful diamonds you're wearing!*

> MAE WEST: *Goodness had nothing to do with it, dearie.*

— NICE ONE —

Comedian **Will Rogers** found that the cinema possessed one overwhelming advantage for the performer:

> *'The movies are the only business where you can go out front and applaud yourself.'*

In his films, bottle-nosed comedian W. C. Fields played The Man You Love To Hate; but author **Leo Rosten** took a charitable view of him:

> *'Anybody who hates children and dogs can't be all bad.'*

Screen hero **Errol Flynn**, whose private life was expensively wild, confessed:

'My problem lies in reconciling my gross habits with my net income.'

Veteran star **Mickey Rooney**'s marital career has been extraordinary even by showbiz standards, as he himself recognizes:

'I'm the only man who has a marriage licence made out To Whom It May Concern.'

n *I'm No Angel*, a reporter asks **Mae West** why she told a court all about the men in her life. Her classic retort:

> *'It's not the men in your life that counts, it's the life in your men.'*

n the Marx Brothers' films **Groucho** was blatantly a crook, a fake, or both at once. Hence this supposed letter to a certain Membership Secretary:

> *'Please accept my resignation. I don't care to belong to a club that will have me as a member.'*

Sam Goldwyn explains why competition from television damaged the film industry so badly:

'Why should people go out and pay money to see bad films when they can stay at home and see bad television for nothing?'

Suave film star **George Sanders**:

'An actor is not quite a human being – but then, who is?'

TAKE THAT!

Dr Samuel Johnson, undisputed king of 18th century English talkers, restrained his usual ferocity when he received a visit from the great actress Mrs Siddons. Since his servant proved slow in bringing her a chair, Johnson made the incident the occasion for a compliment:

'You see, madam, wherever you go, there are no seats to be had.'

D. W. Griffith, director of the epoch-making *Birth of a Nation*, is universally recognized as a pioneer of early film-making. Strangely, he was never invited to leave his footprints in cement outside Grauman's Chinese Restaurant – Hollywood's way of conferring immortality.

Columnist **Hedda Hopper** commented on this oversight in this subtle tribute to a movie giant:

'His footprints were never asked for, yet no one has ever filled his shoes.'

SPOKEN FROM THE ARTS

Critics and playwrights, novelists and poets, painters, composers and dancers all have, in their time, coined or elicited some highly quotable remarks:

A friend found the 18th century playwright **R. B. Sheridan** in the street, glass in hand, watching as his theatre, the Drury Lane, burned down. Sheridan remarked calmly:

'A man may surely be allowed to take a glass of wine by his own fireside.'

The witty **Sydney Smith** claimed that, in his work as a critic:

'I never read a book before reviewing it; it prejudices a man so.'

Drama critic **James Agate** on theatre audiences:

'Long experience has taught me that in England nobody goes to the theatre unless he or she has bronchitis.'

James Agate on actors:

'A professional is a man who can do his job when he doesn't feel like it. An amateur is a man who can't do his job when he does feel like it.'

29

George Bernard Shaw:

> *'A drama critic is a man who leaves no turn unstoned.'*

The book you are now reading is a work of research, as **Wilson Mizner** kindly points out:

> *'When you take stuff from one writer, it's plagiarism; but when you take it from many writers, it's research.'*

Oscar Wilde remained unruffled by the failure of his early play *The Duchess of Padua*:

> *'The play itself was a profound success. But the audience was a profound failure.'*

The biographer is even worse than a critic or an audience, according to **Oscar Wilde**:

> *'Every great man nowadays has his disciples, and it is always Judas who writes the biography.'*

Playwright **John Osborne** turns on the critics:

> *'Asking a working writer what he thinks about critics is like asking a lamp-post what it thinks about dogs.'*

Novelist **Joseph Heller** describes a rugged individualist:

> *'He was a self-made man who owed his lack of success to nobody.'*

Journalist **J. Alfred Spender**:

> *'The misfortune of the "artistic temperament" is that so many people have the temperament and so few the art.'*

Artistic integrity is hard on mothers. **Bernard Shaw** boasted that he allowed his aged parent to support him while he wrote novels that no one would publish:

> *'I did not throw myself into the battle of life: I threw my mother into it.'*

The American writer **William Faulkner** scorned the less sensational art of an earlier American novelist:

> *'Henry James was one of the nicest old ladies I ever met.'*

TAKE THAT!

Confronted with US Customs, **Oscar Wilde** exclaimed with magnificent bravado:

> *'I have nothing to declare – except my genius!'*

SHUCKS!

'Cowboy' humorist **Will Rogers** was the original author of this immortal comment on the Venus de Milo:

'See what'll happen to you if you don't stop biting your finger nails!'

The booklover's worst enemy is the book-borrower. **Sir Walter Scott**:

'I find that though many of my friends are poor arithmeticians, they are nearly all good book-keepers.'

Musician **Pete Seeger**:

> *'Education is when you read the fine print. Experience is what you get if you don't.'*

A character in one of **Christopher Morley**'s novels took an extremely practical view of the dancer's art:

> *'Dancing is a wonderful training for girls; it's the first way you learn to guess what a man is going to do before he does it.'*

Music critic **Ernest Newman** argued that in the arts justice was eventually done:

> *'The good composer is slowly discovered, the bad composer is slowly found out.'*

The American painter **James McNeil Whistler** was witty and also waspish; he wrote a treatise on *The Gentle Art of Making Enemies*. Towards the end of his life he was heard to complain:

> *'I'm lonesome. They are all dying. I have hardly a warm personal enemy left.'*

Dancer and choreographer **Sir Robert Helpman** on the difference between audacity and art:

> *'The trouble with nude dancing is that not everything stops when the music does.'*

LIFE LINES

Reflections on the meaning of life, the universe and everything to do with human behaviour are by no means always serious subjects of conversation, as the following examples illustrate:

Playwright **Tom Stoppard**:

'I think age is a very high price to pay for maturity.'

American **Cardinal Spellman** on old age . . . and beyond:

'You've heard of the three ages of man: youth, age, and ''you are looking wonderful''.'

One day Dr Johnson happened to meet **Oliver Edwards**, a man he had known at college many years before. Unusually, it was not the Sage of Fleet Street who said the memorable thing, but the otherwise unknown Edwards:

'You are a philosopher, Dr Johnson. I have tried, too, in my time to be a philosopher; but, I don't know how, cheerfulness was always breaking in.'

Dean Swift, scathing as ever on the subject of human follies:

'Old men and comets have been reverenced for the same reason: their long beards, and pretences to foretell events.'

Woody Allen:

'I don't want to achieve immortality through my work. I want to achieve it through not dying.'

— NICE ONE —

The artist **Aubrey Beardsley**, darling of the 'camp' 1890s, was consumptive but made light of it:

'Really I believe I'm so affected, even my lungs are affected.'

Premature obituaries get published somehow from time to time. In a cable sent from Europe to the Associated Press news agency after reading of his own demise, **Mark Twain** commented drily:

'The reports of my death are greatly exaggerated.'

American writer **W. D. Howells** anticipated modern science by discovering the time-warp:

'Some people can stay longer in an hour than others can in a week.'

Despite his gift for comedy, **Mark Twain** was a savage
pessimist, as is shown by observations such as:

*'If you pick up a starving dog and make him prosperous, he
will not bite you; that is the principal difference between a
dog and a man.'*

Apparently the great Greek thinker **Socrates** also believed that philosophy and cheerfulness were incompatible. He advised:

'By all means marry: if you get a good wife, you'll be happy; if you get a bad one, you'll become a philosopher.'

Bernard Shaw on English puritanism:

'Morality consists in suspecting other people of not being legally married.'

Dialogue across the centuries:

FRANCIS BACON: *Silence is the virtue of fools.*

ABRAHAM LINCOLN: *Better to remain silent and be thought a fool than to speak out and remove all doubt.*

The quest for universal peace, as seen by **Woody Allen**:

'The lion and the calf shall lie down together, but the calf won't get much sleep.'

Benjamin Disraeli identified a vital symptom of decay:

'When a man fell into his anecdotage it was a sign for him to retire from the world.'

TALKING POLITICS

Politicians are often on the receiving end of wisecracks, but sometimes too they can give as good as they get:

Simon Cameron, a 19th century American politician whose own reputation was somewhat doubtful, took a cynical view of his trade:

> *'An honest politician is one who when he is bought will stay bought.'*

Mark Twain's opinion of his elected representatives was clear enough:

> *'Reader, suppose you were an idiot; and suppose you were a member of Congress; but I repeat myself . . .'*

A man told **Coolidge** that he'd bet a friend he could get more than two words out of the President. Said Coolidge:

> *'You lose.'*

Sir Winston Churchill on the hazards of political life:

> *'Politics are almost as exciting as war. In war you can only be killed once, but in politics many times.'*

Good advice for politicians from American humorist **Josh Billings**:

> *'To enjoy a good reputation, give publicly and steal privately.'*

Calvin Coolidge, President of the United States, was often ridiculed for his taciturn personality. He defended himself by saying that

> *'I have noticed that nothing I never said ever did me any harm.'* GROAN!

American comedian George Burns:

> *'Too bad all the people who know how to run the country are busy driving taxi cabs and cutting hair.'*

Aneurin Bevan, hero of the Left during the 1950s and '60s:

> *'I read the newspaper avidly. It is my one form of continuous fiction.'*

F. E. Smith on Churchillian eloquence:

> *'Winston has devoted the best years of his life to preparing his impromptu speeches.'*

Newspaper reporting has inspired little confidence in those best qualified to judge. American editor **Erwin Knoll**:

'Everything you read in the newspapers is absolutely true except for the rare story of which you happen to have first-hand knowledge.'

Curmudgeonly comedian **W. C. Fields** had a ready answer when asked who he would vote for:

'Hell, I never vote for anybody; I always vote against.'

American President **Harry S. Truman** tells it like it is:

'It's a recession when your neighbour loses his job; it's a depression when you lose your own.'

The American vice-presidency sounds an important office, but in reality the vice-president has virtually no power and few responsibilities. One vice-president, **Thomas R. Marshall**, told the following story:

'Once there were two brothers. One ran away to sea, the other was elected vice-president, and nothing was ever heard of either of them again.'

Will Rogers on income tax:

'It has made more liars out of the American people than Golf.

Most of the world's monarchies have disappeared during the 20th century. On being deposed, **King Farouk** of Egypt remarked:

> *'There will soon be only five kings left: the Kings of England, Diamonds, Hearts, Spades and Clubs.'*

Jean Baptiste Colbert was probably the first minister of finance in the modern sense. He knew exactly what he was doing:

> *'The art of taxation consists in so plucking the goose as to obtain the largest amount of feathers with the least amount of hissing.'*

PROFESSIONAL OPINION

The learned professions have us at their mercy. It is hardly surprising, therefore, if they have occasionally been the targets as well as the authors of various well-chosen words:

Lord Brougham, who became Lord Chancellor, did not think particularly well of his fellow practitioners:

'A lawyer is a learned gentleman who rescues your estate from your enemies and keeps it himself.'

Sir Winston Churchill gives a politician's view of the most prestigious modern profession:

'Scientists should be on tap but not on top.'

Benjamin Franklin warned darkly:

'He's a fool that makes his doctor his heir.'

17th century writer **Francis Quarles** on 'covering up your mistakes':

'Physicians of all men are most happy; what good success soever they have, the world proclaimeth, and what faults they commit, the earth covereth.'

Quarles's contemporary, the physician **Sir Samuel Garth**, admitted in a spirit of self-criticism:

Whilst others meanly asked whole months to slay,
I oft dispatched the patient in a day.

Education. By the 1770s, **Dr Johnson** (himself an ex-schoolmaster) was lamenting the passing of 'the good old days':

'There is less flogging in our great schools than formerly, but then less is learned there; so that what the boys get at one end they lose at the other.'

In the good/bad old days, a man's eldest son inherited his estate, another son went into the army – and the dunce went into the Church. The **Reverend Sydney Smith** pointed out how absurd this was:

'When a man is a fool, in England we only trust him with the immortal concerns of human beings.'

WIT'S END

There have always been people whose every remembered word seems a gem of verbal wizardry. The following enviable quotations are gleaned from the works of such giants of humour:

Sydney Smith was one of the great English wits. One of his typically playful remarks was:

> *'Gout is the only enemy which I don't wish to have at my feet.'*

Smith's wit had a strong vein of fantasy, one example being the way in which he expressed his disapproval of an acquaintance:

> *'He deserves to be preached to death by wild curates.'*

Washington Irving, author of 'Rip Van Winkle':

> *'A sharp tongue is the only edged tool that grows keener with constant use.'*

G. K. Chesterton explains the link between wit and cruelty:

> *'Wit is a sword; it is meant to make people feel the point as well as see it.'*

Sydney Smith was often exasperated by Lord Macaulay, who was a non-stop talker. Smith once told him:

'You know, when I am gone you will be sorry you never heard me speak.'

Smith on Macaulay:

'He has occasional flashes of silence that make his conversation perfectly delightful.'

Sydney Smith on Sydney Smith:

'The whole of my life has been passed like a razor – in hot water or a scrape!'

NICE ONE

17th century humour. **Daniel Purcell**, 'the famous punster', was challenged to make a new pun on the spot.

'Upon what subject?' asked Purcell.
'The King,' ventured his challenger.
'The King, sir,' said Purcell, 'is not a subject.'

The Irish playwright Oscar Wilde remains the most famous of all wits, as one of his modern competitors, **Dorothy Parker**, conceded:

If, with the literate, I am
Impelled to try an epigram,
I never seek to take the credit;
We all assume that Oscar said it.

When a friend gave birth, **Dorothy Parker** sent her a telegram:

'Congratulations: we all knew you had it in you.'

Wilde on travel literature:

'I never travel without my diary. One should always have something sensational to read in the train.'

Oscar Wilde was harshly punished for violating the moral taboos of Victorian England, but his wit remained undimmed. Standing in the pouring rain, handcuffed, on his way to prison, he remarked:

'If this is the way Queen Victoria treats her convicts, she doesn't deserve to have any.'

Oscar Wilde on drink:

'Work is the curse of the drinking classes.'

'Absinthe makes the heart grow fonder.'

Oscar Wilde lectured in the United States – for the money:

'Of course, if one had enough money to go to America, one wouldn't go.'

Wilde found much to entertain him in America, including its myths:

'The youth of America is their oldest tradition. It has been going on now for three hundred years.'

Comic poet **Ogden Nash** knew the way to a girl's heart:

> *Candy is dandy*
> *But liquor is quicker.*

Wilde put this Wildean view of society into the mouth of one of his characters:

> *'To be in it is merely a bore. But to be out of it is simply a tragedy.'*

Much of **Wilde**'s humour is what we should now call 'camp':

> *'I feel that football is all very well as a game for rough girls, but it is hardly suitable for delicate boys.'*

ROMANCE LANGUAGE

The subject of love was bound to come up since it has inspired more speeches than Prime Minister's Question Time – not all of them serious:

American wit Dorothy Parker was disillusioned:

> *By the time you swear you're his,*
> *Shivering and sighing,*
> *And he vows his passion is*
> *Infinite, undying –*
> *Lady, make a note of this:*
> *One of you is lying.*

Readers of a later chapter in this book, 'A Talent to Abuse', will find plenty of ammunition to use against women. **Groucho Marx** answers on their behalf:

'*Anyone who says he can see through women is missing a lot.*'

Actress **Evelyn Laye** believed that sex should be discreet and private:

'*Sex, unlike justice, should not be seen to be done.*'

Once, women were supposed to be indifferent to sex. The actress **Cornelia Otis Skinner** told all:

'Woman's virtue is man's greatest invention.'

By the free and easy 1920s, actress **Tallulah Bankhead** felt able to boast:

'I'm as pure as the driven slush.'

Tallulah Bankhead on starting as you mean to go on:

'The only thing I regret about my past is the length of it. If I had to live my life again I'd make the same mistakes, only sooner.'

Bad girls' seminar:

TALLULAH BANKHEAD: It's the good girls who keep diaries; the bad girls never have the time.

MAE WEST: Keep a diary and one day it'll keep you.

Woody Allen provides a reason for remaining cheerful:

'Love is the answer, but while you are waiting for the answer, sex raises some pretty good questions.'

BOOM!
BOOM!

Woody Allen, 20th century *homo neuroticus*:

   'The difference between sex and death is that with death you can do it alone and no one is going to make fun of you.'

The Kinsey Report was a pioneering investigation of sexual behaviour – but **Dr Kinsey's wife** complained:

   'I don't see so much of Alfred any more since he got so interested in sex.'

Two minds with but a single . . .

   GROUCHO MARX: *A man's only as old as the woman he feels.*

   JEAN HARLOW: *I like to wake up feeling a new man.*

MARRIAGE LINES

If you're not careful, sex can lead to marriage, an institution which has taken plenty of knocks over the centuries. Here are just a few of them!

American writer **Helen Rowland**, one of the wittiest commentators on the battle of the sexes, gives the girl's-eye view:

'*A bachelor never quite gets over the idea that he is a thing of beauty and a boy forever.*'

'*The hardest task in a girl's life is to prove to a man that his intentions are serious.*'

'*When you see what some girls marry, you realize how much they must hate to work for a living.*'

American humorist **James Thurber**:

'*A woman's place is in the wrong.*'

Oscar Wilde describes the mating season:

'The London season is entirely matrimonial; people are either hunting for husbands or hiding from them.'

For women, there is only a choice of evils – according to **Oscar Wilde**:

'Twenty years of romance makes a woman look like a ruin; but twenty years of marriage makes her something like a public building.'

A recent attack from writer **David Pryce-Jones**:

'When you're bored with yourself, marry and be bored with someone else.'

The philosophical view, as expounded by 18th century dramatist George Farquhar:

'Hanging and marriage, you know, go by Destiny.'

Professional cynic **H. L. Mencken**:

'Bachelors know more about women than married men. If they didn't they'd be married too.'

'It is more blessed to give than to receive; for example, wedding presents.'

There are many motives for marrying, and especially for 'marrying well'. American comedian **Joey Adams**:

'The most popular labour-saving device today is still a husband with money.'

GROAN!

Robert Louis Stevenson was no enemy to marriage, which was

'at its lowest . . . a sort of friendship recognized by the police.'

Dr Johnson's verdict on matrimony was favourable – just:

'Marriage has many pains, but celibacy has no pleasures.'

But when a man who had been unhappily married decided to take the plunge again immediately after his first wife's death, **Johnson** said that it represented

'The triumph of hope over experience.'

Poet **William Blake**'s version of 'getting to know each other':

When a man has married a wife, he finds out whether
Her knees and elbows are only glued together.

Benjamin Franklin advised husbands to take a prudent course:

'Keep your eyes wide open before marriage and half-shut afterwards.'

Zsa Zsa Gabor, speaking from experience:

'A girl must marry for love, and keep on marrying until she finds it.'

Oscar Wilde noted that:

'Woman begins by resisting a man's advances and ends by blocking his retreat.'

Canadian humorist **Stephen Leacock**:

'Many a man in love with a dimple makes the mistake of marrying the whole girl.'

The wit **Sydney Smith** neatly pictured the married state:

> *'It resembles a pair of shears, so joined that they cannot be separated; often moving in opposite directions, yet always punishing anyone who comes between them.'*

Clergyman and writer **Charles Colton** describes the worst of matrimonial disappointments:

> *'Marriage is a feast where the grace is sometimes better than the dinner.'*

The poet **Samuel Rogers**:

> *'It doesn't much signify whom one marries, for one is sure to find next morning it was someone else.'*

The poet **Shelley** and more recent author **Norman Douglas** expressed directly opposing opinions – but both managed to complain:

> SHELLEY: *When a man marries, dies, or turns Hindoo, his best friends hear no more of him.*

> DOUGLAS: *Many a man who thinks to found a home discovers that he has merely opened a tavern for his friends.*

The novelist **Samuel Butler**:

> *'Brigands demand your money or your life; women require both.'*

When Brigham Young founded the Mormon community in Utah, polygamy was permitted. The result, said **Artemus Ward**, was that

'The pretty girls in Utah mostly marry Young.'

The marital adventures of Zsa Zsa Gabor and other members of her family often made the headlines. **Oscar Levant** summed up:

'Marriage is for bores. I mean Gabors.'

American politician **Hubert Humphrey** gave a different slant on an old subject:

'Behind every successful man stands a surprised mother-in-law.' BOOM!
BOOM!

Marriage can have serious consequences, as **Mark Twain** observed:

'Familiarity breeds contempt – and children.'

American novelist **Peter De Vries** describes a universal experience:

'There are times when parenthood seems nothing but feeding the mouth that bites you.'

It is said that a man likes nothing better than a 'safely' married woman with whom to indulge in a casual flirtation. That woman's husband may not regard the matter in the same light, however, as **Helen Rowland** observes:

'One man's folly is another man's wife.'

She advised:

'Never trust a husband too far nor a bachelor too near.'

A Mediterranean perspective from **Lord Byron**:

What men call gallantry, and gods adultery
Is much more common where the climate's sultry.

Alexandre Dumas the elder reflects in the urbane French style:

'The chain of wedlock is so heavy that it takes two to carry it, sometimes three.'

Helen Rowland:

'When a girl marries she exchanges the attentions of many men for the inattention of one.'

TAKE THAT!

Lord Mancroft on the properly serviced and run husband:

'Happy the man with a wife to tell him what to do and a secretary to do it for him.'

Dorothy Parker and Robert Benchley only just preserved their virtue – says Parker:

'He and I had an office so tiny that an inch smaller and it would have been adultery.'

The most sophisticated modern society puzzles Cleveland Amory:

'Relations between the sexes are so complicated that the only way you can tell if members of the set are "going together" is if they're married. Then, almost certainly, they are not.'

Is it all worth it? Lord Beaverbrook thought not:

'Buy old masters. They fetch a better price than old mistresses.'

Hollywood star John Barrymore came to see that 'time is money':

'You never realize how short a month is until you pay alimony.'

Anonymous:

'Widows are divided into two classes: the bereaved and the relieved.'

LATE ENTRIES

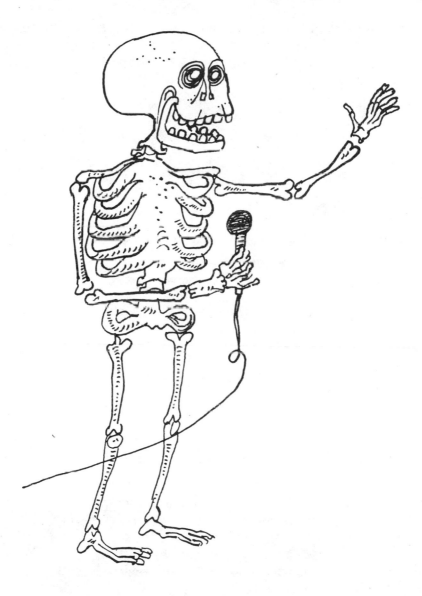

**Epitaphs, inscriptions and verses
in memoriam.**

One of the curses of fame is that someone is sure to score off you by composing a witty epitaph for you . . . even before you're dead.

The Earl of Rochester wrote one on King Charles II, then got drunk and accidentally showed it to his royal master. It read:

> *Here lies our sovereign lord the king*
> *Whose promise none relies on;*
> *Who never said a foolish thing*
> *Nor ever did a wise one.*

The **Merry Monarch** had a ready answer:

> *'This is very true; for my words are my own, and my actions are my ministers.'*

This inscription, commemorating a 17th century author, tells the old, old story of neglected genius:

> *Whilst Butler, needy wretch, was yet alive,*
> *No generous patron would a dinner give.*
> *See him when starved to death and turned to dust*
> *Presented with a monumental bust.*
> *The poet's fate is here in emblem shewn:*
> *He asked for bread, and he received a stone.*

The 18th century writer **Horace Walpole** recorded some verses
that circulated after the death of Frederick, Prince of Wales:

> *Here lies Fred,*
> *Who was alive and is dead:*
> *Had it been his father,*
> *I had much rather;*
> *Had it been his brother,*
> *Still better than another;*
> *Had it been his sister,*
> *No one would have missed her;*
> *Had it been the whole generation,*
> *Still better for the nation;*
> *But since 'tis only Fred,*
> *Who was alive and is dead –*
> *There's no more to be said.*

An anonymous punster commemorated Dr John Potter,
Archbishop of Canterbury:

> *Alack and well a day*
> *Potter himself is turned to clay.*

GROAN!

Lord Byron savaged prime minister William Pitt the Younger,
who was buried in Westminster Abbey:

> *With death doomed to grapple,*
> *Beneath this cold slab, he*
> *Who lied in the chapel*
> *Now lies in the Abbey.*

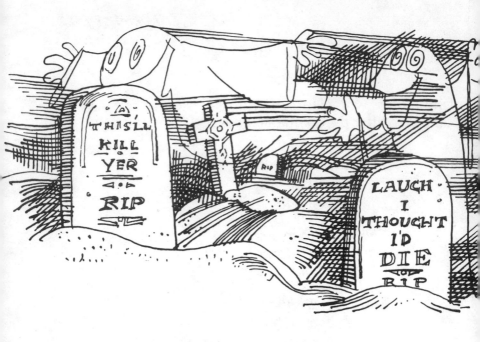

The poet **Ben Jonson**, Shakespeare's contemporary, wrote this vitriolic epitaph for a great lord:

> Here lies a valiant warrior
> Who never drew a sword;
> Here lies a noble courtier
> Who never kept his word;
> Here lies the Earl of Leicester
> Who governed the estates
> Whom the earth could never living love
> And the just heaven now hates.

The 'Welsh Wizard', **David Lloyd George**, suggested an epitaph for himself that might have been adopted by many other politicians:

> Count not my broken pledges as a crime,
> I MEANT them, HOW I meant them, at the time.

64

Wisecracking American writer **Dorothy Parker** proposed this simple tombstone inscription for herself:

Excuse my dust.

Hilaire Belloc wrote of himself with the cheerful vanity of an author:

> *When I am dead, I hope it may be said*
> *'His sins were scarlet but his books were read.'*

John Gay, author of *The Beggars' Opera*, composed his own epitaph:

> *Life is a jest, and all things show it.*
> *I thought so once; but now I know it.*

John Gibson Lockhart, Sir Walter Scott's biographer, suggested this intentionally clumsy verse epitaph for a clumsy would-be poet:

> *Here lies that peerless peer Lord Peter,*
> *Who broke the laws of God and man and metre.*

Oliver Goldsmith was a great writer but a notoriously inept conversationalist. On one occasion the actor **David Garrick** improvised this epitaph for his friend 'Noll':

> *Here lies Nolly Goldsmith, for shortness called Noll,*
> *Who wrote like an angel but talked like poor Poll.*

In this epitaph on himself, the 18th century poet **Matthew Prior** claimed a posthumous equality with the great royal families of Europe:

> *Nobles and heralds by your leave,*
> *Here lies what once was Matthew Prior;*
> *The son of Adam and of Eve –*
> *Can Bourbon or Nassau go higher?*

Shakespeare's tomb at Stratford-on-Avon carries this solemn warning:

> *Good friend, for Jesu's sake forbear*
> *To dig the dust enclosèd here;*
> *Blessed be the man that spares these stones,*
> *And cursed be he that moves my bones.*

The 18th century Scottish philosopher **David Hume** was much concerned with the workings of the human mind — to the very end, as his tomb at Edinburgh demonstrates:

> *Within this circular idea,*
> *Called vulgarly a tomb,*
> *The ideas and impressions lie*
> *That constituted Hume.*

As a young man, still unknown to fame, the great American **Benjamin Franklin** composed this elaborate epitaph for himself:

> *The body of*
> *Benjamin Franklin, printer*
> *(Like the cover of an old book,*
> *Its contents worn out*
> *And stript of its lettering and gilding)*
> *Lies here, food for worms.*
> *Yet the work itself shall not be lost,*
> *For it will, as he believed, appear once more*
> *In a new*
> *And more beautiful edition,*
> *Corrected and amended*
> *By its Author!*

William Blake, eccentric poet and painter, detested everything his highly successful fellow-artist, Sir Joshua Reynolds, stood for. Hence this odd little verse:

When Sir Joshua Reynolds died
All Nature was degraded;
The King dropped a tear in the Queen's ear,
And all his pictures faded.

On **Nance Oldfield**, a famous 18th century actress:

> *This we must own in justice to her shade,*
> *'Tis the first bad exit Oldfield ever made.*

Curmudgeonly comic **W. C. Fields** said that his epitaph should be:

> *On the whole I'd rather be in Philadelphia.*

Groucho Marx had very definite ideas:

> *I want it known here and now that this is what I want on my tombstone. Here lies Groucho Marx, and Lies and Lies and Lies and Lies. P. S. He never kissed an ugly girl.*

Versatile Hollywood actor **Lionel Barrymore** told a magazine that his epitaph should be:

> *Well, I've played everything but a harp.*

The 18th century actor **Samuel Foote**, a brilliant mimic, inspired two understandably anonymous tributes:

> *Foote from his earthly stage, alas! is hurled;*
> *Death took him off, who took off all the world.*

and

> *Here lies one Foote, whose death may thousands serve,*
> *For death has now one foot within the grave.*

The poet Keats proposed for his epitaph the gloomy 'Here lies one whose name was writ in water.' The scandalous **Robert Ross,** Oscar Wilde's intimate friend, went one better on his own behalf:

> *Here lies one whose name is writ in hot water!*

No guarantee of authenticity is offered for this classically brief gravestone inscription:

> *Cheerio, see you soon.*

Graveyard philosophy from the USA:

> *Once I wasn't*
> *Then I was*
> *Now I ain't again.*

A young person's tale:

> *Came in*
> *Looked about*
> *Didn't like it*
> *Went out*

Silly, but brief:

> *Here lies Ann Mann;*
> *She lived an old maid*
> *And she died an old Mann.*

This 18th century tombstone tribute is unintentionally funny:

> Today he rises from a Velvet Bed
> Tomorrow he's in one that's made of Lead
>
> Today perfumed, and sweet as is the Rose,
> Tomorrow stinks in ev'ry Body's Nose

A missionary in India was accidentally shot by his native bearer. His tombstone is said to have included the hardly appropriate Biblical quotation:

> 'Well done thou good and faithful servant.'

An Irish epitaph:

> Erected in the memory of
> John Philips
> Accidentally shot
> As a mark of affection by his brother.

From Dumfries:

> Here lies Andrew MacPherson,
> Who was a peculiar person;
> He stood six foot two
> Without his shoe,
> And he was slew
> At Waterloo.

These tombstones are less than fulsome in praise of the dear departed . . .

> Friend, in your epitaph I'm grieved
> So very much is said:
> One half will never be believed,
> The other never read.

> Here lies John Rackett
> In his wooden jacket;
> He kept neither horses nor mules.
> He lived like a hog
> And died like a dog,
> And left all his money to fools.

Anna Harrison of Easingwold in Yorkshire had *some* good qualities:

> Her tongue and her hands were not governable,
> But the rest of her members she kept in subjection.

From Yarmouth:

> Owen Moore has gone away,
> Owin' more than he can pay.

From Shrewsbury:

> Here lies the body of Martha Dias,
> Who was always uneasy and not over pious;
> She lived to the age of threescore and ten,
> And gave that to the worms she refused to the men.

It would be nice to know just who **Hilaire Belloc** had in mind
when he penned this:

> *Here richly, with ridiculous display,*
> *The Politician's corpse was laid away.*
> *While all of his acquaintance sneered and slanged,*
> *I wept: for I had longed to see him hanged.*

There are other versions of this one, naming other towns — not surprisingly, since it bursts with civic pride:

> *Here lie the bones of Elizabeth Charlotte,*
> *Born a virgin, died a harlot.*
> *She was aye a virgin at seventeen,*
> *A remarkable thing in Aberdeen.*

Dorothy Parker, bitchy as always, suggested that this should be carved on an actress's tombstone:

> *Her name, cut clear upon this marble cross,*
> *Shines, as it shone when she was still on earth,*
> *While tenderly the mild, agreeable moss*
> *Obscures the figures of her date of birth.*

One American Congressman (**Samuel Cox**) seeing off another:

> *Beneath this stone Owen Lovejoy lies,*
> *Little in everything except in size;*
> *What though his burly body fills the hole,*
> *Yet through Hell's keyhole crept his little soul.*

The journalist **George Augustus Sala** dealt a cruel posthumous blow to a colleague, John Camden Hotten:

> *Hotten*
> *Rotten*
> *Forgotten*

This marital last word has been attributed to the poet **John Dryden**:

> *Here lies my wife: here let her lie!*
> *Now she's at rest, and so am I.*

One version of a popular and vindictive adieu runs as follows:

> *My wife lies dead, yes here she lies;*
> *Nobody laughs and nobody cries.*
> *Where she has gone to and how she fares*
> *Nobody knows and nobody cares.*

A formula for happiness (eventual) in marriage:

> *Underneath this tuft doth lie,*
> *Back to back, my wife and I.*
> *Generous stranger, spare a tear,*
> *For could she speak, I cannot hear.*
> *Happier far than when in life,*
> *Free from noise and free from strife,*
> *When the last trump the air doth fill,*
> *If she gets up then I'll lie still.*

On tombstones, at least, men seem to get the better of the battle of the sexes. But there are exceptions:

> *Here lies the mother of children seven,*
> *Four on earth and three in heaven;*
> *The three in heaven preferring rather*
> *To die with mother than live with father.*

The moral of this is 'better the devil you *don't* know':

> *Here lies Mary, the wife of John Ford,*
> *We hope her soul is gone to the Lord;*
> *But if for Hell she has changed this life*
> *She had better be there than be John Ford's wife.*

The poet **Lord Byron** wrote a number of harsh epitaphs – and this single kindly one:

> *Near this spot are deposited the remains of one who possessed Beauty without Vanity, Strength without Insolence, Courage without Ferocity, and all the virtues of Man, without his Vices. This Praise, which would be unmeaning Flattery if inscribed over human ashes is but just tribute to the memory of Boatswain, a Dog.*

Graveyard humour is often excruciating – and never more so than in this epitaph for one 'Cookhouse Jake':

> *Peace to his hashes.*

Lament for a Liverpool brewer:

> *Poor John Scott lies buried here,*
> *Though once he was hale and stout;*
> *Death stretched him on his bitter bier:*
> *In another world he hops about.*

Epitaph for a peer caught cheating at cards:

Here lies
Henry William, twenty-second Lord _____,
In joyful expectation of the last trump.

From Ireland:

Here lie the remains of John Hall, grocer.
The world is not worth a fig
And I have good raisins for saying so.

GROAN!

From the USA:

> *Under the sod and under these trees,*
> *Here lies the body of Solomon Pease.*
> *He's not in this hole but only his pod:*
> *He shelled out his soul and went up to God.*

On a dentist:

> Stranger, approach this spot with gravity:
> John Brown is filling his last cavity.

Epitaph for a hard-drinking carrier, possibly written by **Lord Byron**:

> John Adams lies here, of the parish of Southwell,
> A carrier who carried his can to his mouth well.
> He carried so much, and he carried so fast,
> He could carry no more – so was carried at last;
> For the liquor he drank, being too much for one,
> He could not carry off – so he's now carrion.

78

If your trade is dyeing cloth – this is the sort of epitaph you can expect:

> Here lies a man who first did dye
> When he was twenty-four;
> And yet he lived to reach the age
> Of hoary years fourscore.
> But now he's gone, and certain 'tis
> He'll not dye any more.

On the tomb of a **Mrs Stone** at Melton Mowbray:

> Curious enough we all must say,
> That what was stone should now be clay;
> Most curious still, to own we must,
> That what was stone must soon be dust.

Many epitaphs touch upon the trade followed by the late lamented during his earthly life. This one even includes some discreet advertising:

> Beneath this stone, in hopes of Zion,
> Doth lie the landlord of The Lion.
> His son keeps on the business still
> Resigned unto the heavenly will.

A sexton gets his come uppance:

> Hurrah! My brave boys,
> Let's rejoice at his fall!
> For if he'd have lived
> He'd have buried us all.

In folklore, *all* lawyers are crooks. Hence the note of surprise in this memorial:

> *Here lies one, believe it if you can,*
> *Who, though an attorney, was an honest man.*

And in this, of **Sir John Strange**:

> *Here lies an honest lawyer:*
> *That is Strange!*

TAKE THAT!

Of a first lieutenant of marines, off-duty in Yorkshire:

> *Confined in earth in narrow borders,*
> *He rises not till further orders.*

This 17th century locksmith was clearly a conscientious worker:

> *A zealous locksmith died of late,*
> *And did arrive at Heaven's gate.*
> *He stood without, and would not knock,*
> *Because he meant to pick the lock.*

Robert Trollope of Gateshead was an architect:

> *Here lies Robert Trollope,*
> *Who made yon stones roll up.*
> *When Death took his soul up*
> *His body filled this hole up.*

Inscription for a fisherman who . . . exaggerated:

> *He angled many a purling brook,*
> *But lacked the angler's skill:*
> *He lied about the fish he took,*
> *And here he's lying still.*

Western epitaph for one who knew both sides of a job:

> *Here lies Wild Bill Britt.*
> *Ran for sheriff in '82;*
> *Ran from sheriff in '83;*
> *Buried in '84.*

A wry, graceful farewell from Ashover in Derbyshire:

> *To the memory of*
> *David Wall,*
> *whose superior performance on the*
> *bassoon endeared him to an*
> *extensive musical acquaintance.*
> *His social life closed on the*
> *4th Dec., 1796, in his 57th year.*

From Whitby:

> *Sudden and unexpected was the end*
> *Of our esteemed and beloved friend:*
> *He gave all his friends a sudden shock*
> *By one day falling into Sunderland dock.*

One of **Leonard Robbins'** *Epitaphs for the Speed Age*, with a wide potential application:

> Stranger, pause and shed a tear
> For one who leaves no mourners.
> D. F. Sapp reposes here:
> He would cut corners.

Mini-novel by the American poet **Carl Sandburg**:

> Papa loved mamma
> Mamma loved men
> Mamma's in the graveyard
> Papa's in the pen.

Dr Johnson had no doubts about the final destination of a recently deceased gentleman from Jamaica:

> *'He will not, whither he is now gone, find much difference, I believe, either in the climate or the company.'*

Advice from beyond the grave — to be precise, from Eastwell in Kent:

> *Fear God*
> *Keep the Commandments*
> *and*
> *Don't attempt to climb a tree,*
> *For that's what caused the death of me.*

A comment on 'death after death'; from Kingsbridge in Devon:

> *Here lie I at the Chancel door.*
> *Here I lie because I'm poor.*
> *The further in the more you pay;*
> *Here lie I as warm as they.*

From Leeds:

> *Angels, grant a trifling boon*
> *To our brother who here lies.*
> *Sound the trumpet after noon,*
> *Earlier doth he never rise.*

Epitaph possibly written by **Oliver Goldsmith**:

> *Here lies poor Ned Pardon, from misery freed,*
> *Who long was a bookseller's hack;*
> *He led such a damnable life in this world,*
> *I don't think he'll ever come back.*

Wolverhampton, 1690:

> *Here lies the bones*
> *Of Joseph Jones,*
> *Who ate while he was able;*
> *But once o'erfed,*
> *He dropped down dead*
> *And fell beneathe the table.*
> *When from the tomb*
> *To meet his doom,*
> *He rises amidst the sinners,*
> *Since he must dwell*
> *In Heaven or Hell,*
> *Take him – which gives best dinners.*

A vicar's widow, questioned about her spouse's recent passage from Earth to Elsewhere, replied:

> *'I'm sure my husband is enjoying eternal bliss. But must we talk about such an unpleasant subject?'*

Sad story from Norfolk:

> *Here lie I and my four daughters,*
> *Killed by drinking Cheltenham waters.*
> *Had we but stuck to Epsom Salts,*
> *We wouldn't be lying in these here vaults.*

From Ryde, Isle of Wight:

> *There was an old lady from Ryde*
> *Who ate some apples and died.*
> *The apples fermented inside the lamented*
> *Made cider inside her inside.* — *NICE ONE*

Bad news from Bideford:

> *The wedding day appointed was,*
> *The wedding clothes provided.*
> *But ere the day did come, alas,*
> *He sickened, and he dieded.*

The 19th century children's writer **George Macdonald** composed the ultimate plea for mutual tolerance:

> *Here lie I, Martin Elginbrodde:*
> *Hae mercy o' my soul, Lord God;*
> *As I wad do, were I Lord God,*
> *And ye were Martin Elginbrodde.*

85

DEFINITIVELY SPEAKING

Extraordinary and ingenious definitions of familiar words.

DICTIONARY

OF

ALTERNATIVE MEANINGS

Giving the Sources and Originators
of Definitions
in Uncommon Use

by

Nick Harris

Acquaintance A person whom we know well enough to borrow from but not well enough to lend to.

(Ambrose Bierce, US author, 1842-1914?)

Actor An actor's a guy who if you ain't talking about him, he ain't listening. *(Marlon Brando)*

Armour The kind of clothing worn by a man whose tailor is a blacksmith. *(Ambrose Bierce)*

Atheist An atheist is a man who has no invisible means of support. *(John Buchan)*

Baby A loud noise at one end and no sense of responsibility at the other.

(Father Ronald Knox, English author and translator, 1888-1957)

Bachelor A man who never makes the same mistake once.

(Ed Wynn, 20th century US comedian)

Bank A bank is a place where they lend you an umbrella in fair weather and ask for it back when it begins to rain.
(Robert Frost, US poet, 1874-1963)

A bank is a place that will lend you money if you can prove that you don't need it. *(Bob Hope)*

Bigamist A man who marries a beautiful girl and a good cook.
(Chicago Herald-American)

Bore A bore is a man who, when you ask him how he is, tells you.
(Bert Leston Taylor, 20th century US writer)

A person who talks when you wish him to listen. *(Ambrose Bierce)*

Brain The apparatus with which we think we think.
(Ambrose Bierce)

Breeding Good breeding consists in concealing how much we think of ourselves and how little we think of the other person.
(Mark Twain)

Calamity Calamities are of two kinds: misfortune to ourselves, and good fortune to others. *(Ambrose Bierce)*

Cannibal A guy who goes into a restaurant and orders the waiter. *(Jack Benny)*

Caricature Caricature is the tribute mediocrity pays to genius.
(Oscar Wilde)

Celebrity A celebrity is a person who works hard all his life to become known, then wears dark glasses to avoid being recognized. *(Fred Allen, 20th century US comedian)*

Classic A classic is something that everybody wants to have read and nobody wants to read. *(Mark Twain)*

Committee A committee is a group that keeps the minutes and loses hours. *(Milton Berle, 20th century US comedian)*

Conclusion A conclusion is the place where you get tired of thinking. *(Arthur Bloch, 20th century US writer)*

Conference A conference is a gathering of important people who singly can do nothing, but together can decide that nothing can be done. *(Fred Allen)*

Confidence Confidence is simply that quiet assured feeling you have before you fall flat on your face.
(Dr L. Binder, 19th century US historian)

Conscience Conscience is the inner voice which warns us that someone might be looking.
(H. L. Mencken, 20th century US humorist and author)

Cult A cult is a religion with no political power.
(Tom Wolfe, 20th century US author)
. . . It just means not enough people to make a minority.
(Robert Altman, 20th century US film director)

Cynic A blackguard whose faulty vision sees things as they are, not as they ought to be. *(Ambrose Bierce)*

A man who knows the price of everything and the value of nothing. *(Oscar Wilde)*

Dancing Dancing is a perpendicular expression of a horizontal desire. *(Anonymous)*

Débâcle Defeat at cricket and tennis.
(J. B. Morton, alias 20th century humorist 'Beachcomber')

Democracy Democracy is a form of religion. It is the worship of jackals by jackasses. *(H. L. Mencken)*

Diagnosis The physician's art of determining the condition of the patient's purse in order to find out how sick to make him.
(Ambrose Bierce)

Diplomat A diplomat is a man who always remembers a woman's birthday but never remembers her age. *(Robert Frost)*

Economy Cutting down other people's wages. *(J. B. Morton)*

Editor An editor is one who separates the wheat from the chaff and prints the chaff. *(Adlai Stevenson, US politician, 1900-1965)*

Egotist A person of low taste, more interested in himself than in me. *(Ambrose Bierce)*

Epigram Any sentence spoken by anybody who is in the public eye at the moment. *(J. B. Morton)*

Epitaph A belated advertisement for a line of goods that has been permanently discontinued.
(Irvin S. Cobb, 20th century US writer)

A monumental inscription designed to remind the deceased of what he might have been if he had had the will and opportunity.
(Ambrose Bierce)

Expert An expert is one who knows more and more about less and less. *(Nicholas Murray Butler, US educator, 1862-1947)*

An expert is a man who has made all the mistakes which can be made, in a narrow field. *(Niels Bohr, 20th century Danish physicist)*

Faith It was the schoolboy who said, 'Faith is believing what you know ain't so.' *(Mark Twain)*

Fiction The good end happily and the bad unhappily. That is what Fiction means. *(Oscar Wilde)*

Friends

Friends People who borrow books and set wet glasses on them.
(Edwin Arlington Robinson, 20th century US poet)

Friendship Friendship is like money, easier made than kept.
(Samuel Butler, English writer 1835-1902)

Friendship is more tragic than love. It lasts longer. *(Oscar Wilde)*

Future That period of time in which our affairs prosper, our friends are true and our happiness is assured. *(Ambrose Bierce)*

Gambling The sure way of getting nothing for something.
(Wilson Mizner, 20th century US wit)

Genius Genius is born, not paid. *(Oscar Wilde)*

A genius is one who can do anything except make a living.
(Joey Adams, 20th century US comedian)

Gesticulation Any movement made by a foreigner.
(J. B. Morton)

Gossip Gossip is the art of saying nothing in a way that leaves practically nothing unsaid.
(Walter Winchell, 20th century US columnist)

Grand Old Man That means on our continent [North America] anyone with snow-white hair who has kept out of jail till eighty.
(Stephen Leacock, Canadian humorist and author, 1869-1944)

Home Home is the place where, when you have to go there, they have to take you in. *(Robert Frost)*

Imitation Imitation is the sincerest form of flattery.
(Oscar Wilde)

Imitation is the sincerest form of television. *(Fred Allen)*

Jury A jury consists of twelve persons chosen to decide who has the better lawyer. *(Robert Frost)*

Liberal A liberal is a man too broad-minded to take his own side in a quarrel. *(Robert Frost)*

Liberty One of Imagination's most precious possessions.
(Ambrose Bierce)

Life Life is rather like a tin of sardines: we're all of us looking for the key. *(Alan Bennett,* Beyond the Fringe*)*

Life is not a spectacle or a feast; it is a predicament.
(George Santayana, Spanish-American philosopher, 1863-1952)

Life is an incurable disease. *(Abraham Cowley, poet, 1618-1667)*

Life is just one damned thing after another.
(Kin Hubbard, US humorist, 1859-1915)

Life is the art of drawing sufficient conclusions from insufficient premises. *(Samuel Butler)*

Life's a pudding full of plums.
(W. S. Gilbert, English lyricist and poet, 1836-1911)

Logic

Logic Logic is the art of going wrong with confidence.
(Joseph Wood Krutch, 20th century US scholar and critic)

Love A temporary insanity curable by marriage. *(Ambrose Bierce)*
An abject intercourse between tyrants and slaves.
(Oliver Goldsmith, poet, 1728-1774)
Love is like linen often changed, the sweeter.
(Phineas Fletcher, poet, 1582-1650)
Love is like the measles; we all have to go through it.
(Jerome K. Jerome)

Man A creature made at the end of a week's work when God was tired. *(Mark Twain)*

Marriage A community consisting of a master, a mistress and two slaves, making in all two. *(Ambrose Bierce)*
Marriage is a romance in which the hero dies in the first chapter.
(Anonymous)
Marriage is give and take. You'd better give it to her or she'll take it anyway. *(Joey Adams)*
Marriage is like a cage; one sees the birds outside desperate to get in, and those inside equally desperate to get out.
(Michel de Montaigne, French writer, 1533-1592)

Memoirs When you put down the good things you ought to have done, and leave out the bad ones you did do – that's Memoirs.
(Will Rogers, 20th century US comedian)

Monogamy An obsolete word meaning a fidelity complex.
(J. B. Morton)

Moral indignation Moral indignation is jealousy with a halo.
(H. G. Wells)

Nation A nation is a society united by a delusion about its ancestry and by a common hatred of its neighbours.
(Dean Inge, dean of St Paul's, London, 1911-34)

Opera Opera is when a guy gets stabbed in the back and instead of bleeding, he sings. *(Ed Gardner, 20th century US comedian)*

Optimist An optimist is a guy who has never had much experience. *(Don Marquis, 20th century US satirist)*

An optimist is always broke. *(Kin Hubbard)*

A man who gets treed by a lion but enjoys the scenery.
(Walter Winchell)

An optimist is a fellow who believes what's going to be will be postponed. *(Kin Hubbard)*

Originality Originality is the fine art of remembering what you hear but forgetting where you heard it.
(Laurence Peter, 20th century Canadian writer)

Patriotism The last refuge of the scoundrel. *(Dr Johnson)*

Patriotism is your conviction that this country is superior to all others because you were born in it. *(Bernard Shaw)*

Patron Commonly a wretch who supports with insolence, and is paid with flattery. *(Dr Johnson)*

Pessimist A pessimist is someone who, if he is in the bath, will not get out to answer the telephone. *(Quentin Crisp)*

A pessimist is a man who looks both ways when he's crossing the street. *(Laurence Peter)*

The optimist sees the doughnut, the pessimist sees the hole.
(Anonymous)

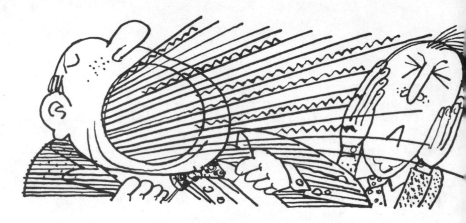

Politician A politician is a man who approaches every question with an open mouth. *(Adlai Stevenson)*

A politician is an animal which can sit on a fence and yet keep both ears to the ground. *(H. L. Mencken)*

The most successful politician is he who says what everybody is thinking most often and in the loudest voice.
(Theodore Roosevelt, US president 1901-9)

Prodigy A child who plays the piano when he ought to be in bed. *(J. B. Morton)*

A child who knows as much when it is a child as it does when it grows up. *(Will Rogers)*

Professor A professor is one who talks in someone else's sleep.
(W. H. Auden)

Psychiatrist A psychiatrist is a man who goes to the Folies-Bergère and looks at the audience.
(Mervyn Stockwood, Bishop of Southwark)

They say a psychiatrist is a fellow who asks you a lot of expensive questions your wife asks for nothing. *(Joey Adams)*

Punctuality Punctuality is something that if you have it, there's often no one around to share it with you.
(Hylda Baker, 20th century English comedienne)

Radical A radical is a man with both feet planted firmly in the air. *(Franklin D. Roosevelt)*

Religion The religion of one age is the literary entertainment of the next. *(Ralph Waldo Emerson, US writer)*
One's religion is whatever he is most interested in.
(J. M. Barrie, author of Peter Pan*)*

Revolution In politics, an abrupt change in the form of misgovernment. *(Ambrose Bierce)*

Robbery Any price charged for any article abroad.
(J. B. Morton)

Sex Sex is an emotion in motion. *(Mae West)*

Success The one unpardonable sin against one's fellows.
(Ambrose Bierce)

Teacher He who can, does. He who cannot, teaches.
(Bernard Shaw)

Television A medium. So called because it is neither rare nor well done. *(Ernie Kovacs, 20th century US film actor)*
A device that permits people who haven't anything to do to watch people who can't do anything. *(Fred Allen)*

Time That which man is always trying to kill, but which ends in killing him. *(Herbert Spencer, English philosopher, 1820-1903)*

Wickedness Wickedness is a myth invented by good people to account for the curious attractiveness of others. *(Oscar Wilde)*

Year A period of three hundred and sixty-five disappointments.
(Ambrose Bierce)

CRACKS OF DOOM

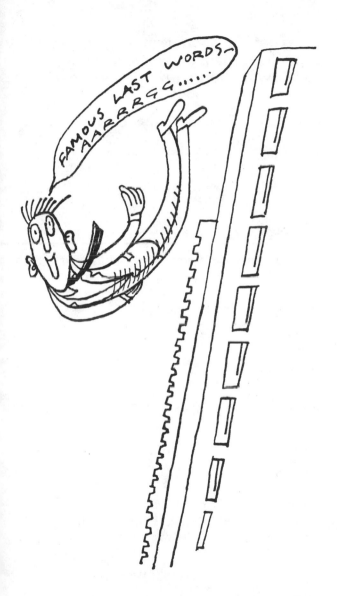

Last words of the great and famous.

We should all like to get in a good parting shot, and many well-known people have managed to do just that . . . or have had 'famous last words' invented for them.

King Charles II expired with exquisite politeness, saying:

> *'I have been a most unconscionable time a-dying, but I hope you will excuse it.'*

According to another account his last thoughts were of his mistress, Nell Gwynne:

> *'Let not poor Nellie starve!'*

Lord Palmerston, twice British prime minister, was witty to the last:

> *'Die, my dear doctor! That's the* last *thing I shall do!'*

When his nurse assured visitors that the patient was somewhat better, the Norwegian dramatist **Henrik Ibsen** growled:

> *'On the contrary.'*

He then proved himself right by promptly expiring.

George IV was evidently taken by surprise, calling to his page:

'Wally, what is this? It is death, my boy. They have deceived me.'

There are several versions of **George V**'s last words, including the solemn 'How is the Empire?' A less reverent story is that, when told he would soon be well enough to visit his favourite resort, the King answered:

'Bugger Bognor.'

When **Disraeli** was dying, he was asked whether he would like Queen Victoria to visit him. The ex-prime minister replied:

'No, it is better not. She would only ask me to take a message to Albert.'

Nero, Emperor of Rome in the first century AD, died as he had lived — with delusions of grandeur. Facing defeat and humiliation as revolt and insurrection raged around him, he committed suicide, exclaiming as he did so:

'What an artist the world is losing in me!'

The poet **Alexander Pope** wrote, towards the end of his final illness:

'Here am I, dying of a hundred good symptoms.'

Finding her family gathered round her bedside during her last illness, **Lady Astor** asked:

'*Am I dying or is this my birthday?*'

After their deaths, Roman emperors were officially recognized as divinities. But they were still reluctant to go. The **Emperor Vespasian** groaned:

'*Dammit — I think I'm becoming a god.*'

Lou Costello, the fat member of the Abbott and Costello comedy partnership, said:

'That was the best ice cream soda I ever tasted.'

Humphrey Bogart remained true to his tough-guy image. His last words are supposed to have been:

'I should never have switched from Scotch to Martinis.'

Dr Joseph Green, a 19th century surgeon, adopted a briskly scientific approach to his own case. He took his own pulse, uttered a single word:

'Stopped.'

Then he fell dead.

NICE ONE

John Philpot Curran, a famous Irish wit, was told by his doctor that he was coughing with more difficulty. Curran's answer was:

'That is surprising, since I have been practising all night.'

The French author **Paul Claudel** was one of those who suspected that Something He Had Eaten had hastened his end. He asked:

'Doctor, do you think it could have been the sausage?'

Richard Monckton Milnes, in his day a noted society man and diner-out, realized that the self-indulgence of a lifetime might have had something to do with his demise. He remarked:

'My exit is the result of too many entrées.'

Like many other patients, the world-conquering **Alexander the Great** blamed the medics:

'I am dying with the help of too many physicians.'

William Pitt the Younger was Britain's prime minister during the long wars against Napoleonic France. When he died, at a moment of crisis, he is said to have spoken these noble words: 'My country! My country! How I leave my country!'

But it was widely believed that this 'official' version was wrong, and that what Pitt actually said was:

'I think I could eat one of Bellamy's veal pies.'

Traditional last words on 'death row' in US prisons:

'Give me some bicarb, warden, I'm gonna have some gas.'

Anton Chekhov, Russian author of bittersweet stories and plays, emptied a sparkling glass, commented

'It's a long time since I have drunk champagne,'

and spoke no more.

The hell-raising Welsh poet **Dylan Thomas** boasted:

'I've had eighteen straight whiskies – I think that's the record.'

The witty and fantastic **Reverend Sydney Smith** died as a result of accidentally drinking some ink. His last words:

'Bring me all the blotting paper there is in the house!'

CRACKS OF DOOM

The wife of the German poet **Heinrich Heine** urged him to beg for God's forgiveness. Heine retorted loftily:

'God will forgive me: that's His trade.'

When a priest came in to see the American wit **Wilson Mizner**, the dying man revived long enough to make a last crack:

'Why should I talk to you? I've just been talking to your boss.'

William Palmer – 'Palmer the poisoner' – was caught, convicted and sentenced. About to step on to the scaffold, he enquired:

'Are you sure it's safe?'

American criminal **James W. Rodgers**, facing a firing squad, was asked whether he had a last request.

'Why yes – a bullet-proof vest.'

Jonathan Swift, author of *Gulliver's Travels*, lay dying when he heard that the composer Handel had come to visit him. Swift called out:

'Ah, a German and a genius – a prodigy! Admit him!

The American poet **Kenneth Rexroth** remembered his father's last days:

> *'He said he was dying of fast women, slow horses, crooked cards and straight whisky.'*

According to the actor and comedian **Kenneth Williams**, this is a true story.

During a performance of a play, actor A was supposed to take out a gun and shoot actor B. When the moment came, A discovered that he had no gun.

In a state of panic, he could think of nothing better than to *kick* B.

In an inspired improvisation, B sank to the ground, gasping:

> *'The boot . . . was poisoned!'*

Gertrude Stein, American experimental writer, asked, 'What *is* the answer?'

Evidently none came, whereupon she laughed and said:

'In that case, what is the question?'

Then she died.

The actor **John Palmer** died on stage with superb timing, having just uttered the line

'There is another and a better world.'

Bing Crosby, Hollywood comedian and 'crooner' beloved of millions, collapsed and died after a friendly eighteen holes at his local club. His last words were happy:

'That was a great game of golf, fellers.'

The French writer **Bernard de Fontenelle** was a hundred years old when he died in 1757, as tranquilly as he had lived. He explained:

'I do not suffer at all, but I do experience a certain difficulty in continuing to exist.'

James Quin, 18th century actor, played the good trooper:

'I could wish this tragic scene were over, but I hope to go through it with becoming modesty.'

The novelist **W. Somerset Maugham**:

'Dying is a very dull, dreary affair. My advice to you is to have nothing to do with it.'

A dramatist proffered his latest work to the French critic **Nicolas Boileau**, presumably unaware of the seriousness of his current illness. Boileau's last words on earth were:

'Do you wish to hasten my last hour?'

American essayist **Logan Pearsall Smith**:

'Thank heaven, the sun has gone in, and I don't have to go out and enjoy it.' GROAN!

The great Scottish economist **Adam Smith**'s last words were unintentionally macabre. He told his colleagues:

'I believe we must adjourn the meeting to some other place.'

On his deathbed the American publisher **Andrew Bradford** was conscious of his failings. A newspaperman to the last, he cried:

'Lord, forgive the errata!'

During the American Civil War, Union **General John Sedgwick** peered over the parapet at the enemy lines, answering friendly warnings with the assertion:

'They couldn't hit an elephant at this dist--'

Lord Holland, expecting an acquaintance with rather morbid tastes, issued this final instruction:

'If Mr Selwyn calls, let him in. If I am alive I shall be very glad to see him, and if I am dead he will be very glad to see me.'

The Russian poet **Vladimir Mayakovsky** killed himself, but observed in his suicide note:

'I don't recommend it for others.'

110

During the French Revolution a condemned *aristo* was offered a last drink on the scaffold. He refused it, saying:

'I lose all sense of direction when I'm drunk.'

The fabulously rich **William H. Vanderbilt** died after remarking that

'I have had no real gratification or enjoyment of any sort more than my neighbour down the block who is worth only . . . half a million.'

At the end of his life **Oscar Wilde** was bankrupt. When told how expensive an operation would be, he remarked:

'Ah well, I suppose I shall have to die beyond my means.'

When the American Revolutionary soldier **Ethan Allen** was told that the angels were waiting for him, he snapped:

'Waiting, are they? Well, let 'em wait!'

Karl Marx:

'Get out! Last words are for fools who haven't already said enough!'

A TALENT TO ABUSE

**A compendium of insult,
scorn and criticism.**

A TALENT TO ABUSE

It is perhaps a sad reflection on human nature, but certainly a happy truth for the collector of prize put-downs, that we are generally better at insulting than at praising our fellow man. Although some of the following were impromptu remarks, the insult is usually all the better for being long premeditated, for as the poet Byron explains:

Now hatred is by far the longest pleasure;
Men love in haste, but they detest at leisure.

PURELY PERSONAL

To begin with, a few brutal examples of crushing retorts by some real pro's:

W. S. Gilbert, writer of the Gilbert and Sullivan operettas, had this to say about some mercifully anonymous acquaintance:

'No one can have a higher opinion of him than I have; and I think he is a dirty little beast.'

Dorothy Parker in a (for her) mildly critical mood:

'She tells enough white lies to ice a cake.'

Heinrich Heine, the author of exquisite lyrics, could be cruelly witty:

> *'She resembles the Venus de Milo: she is very old, has no teeth, and has white spots on her yellow skin.'*

The writer **Virginia Woolf** wrote with inverted snobbery of

> *'Those comfortably padded lunatic asylums which are known euphemistically as the stately homes of England.'*

A profound piece of observation quoted by the writer **C. S. Lewis**:

> *'She's the sort of woman who lives for others – you can tell the others by their hunted expressions.'*

An example of the unintentional insult: Dining with King George V, a cabinet minister declined the offer of a cigar, saying:

> *'No thank you, I only smoke on special occasions.'*

Voltaire, the wittiest of all French writers, sums up the rewards of a successful career as a literary scourge:

> *'My prayer to God is a very short one: ''O Lord, make my enemies ridiculous.'' God has granted it.'*

Sheer bitchiness from Hollywood star **Bette Davis**, describing a starlet:

'There goes the good time that was had by all.'

A TALENT TO ABUSE

An interesting character trait, noted by **Dorothy Parker**:

'That woman can speak eighteen languages, and she can't say No in any of them.'

When a woman told **Sir Winston Churchill** he was drunk, he retorted:

'Madame, you're ugly. Tomorrow morning, however, I shall be sober . . .'

When a flatterer laughed once too often at **Dr Johnson**'s sayings, the Sage crushed him with:

> *'What provokes you to risibility, Sir? Have I said anything that you understand? Then I ask the pardon of the rest of the company.'*

A woman who was too complimentary to **Johnson** was told:

> *'Madam, before you flatter a man so grossly to his face, you should consider whether or not your flattery is worth his having.'*

Johnson mauls an absent acquaintance:

> *'A fellow who makes no figure in company, and has a mind as narrow as the neck of a vinegar cruet.'*

Dr Johnson on the actor Thomas Sheridan:

> *'Why, Sir, Sherry is dull, naturally dull; but it must have taken a great deal of pains to become what we now see him. Such an excess of stupidity, Sir, is not in Nature.'*

As a practitioner of the art of the insult, New York poet and journalist **Dorothy Parker** was almost unrivalled. She particularly detested the socialite and the diplomat Clare Boothe Luce, and when told that Luce was invariably kind to her inferiors, asked:

'Where does she find them?'

When the two women happened to meet in front of a door, **Clare Boothe Luce** indicated that Dorothy Parker should go first, saying 'Age before beauty!' Parker swept through, retorting:

'Pearls before swine.'

Jumper-to-jumper followed by bumper-to-bumper? **Dorothy Parker** speculated:

'If all the girls attending the Yale Prom were laid end to end, I wouldn't be at all surprised.'

In a competition to decide the supreme master of the insult, Dr Johnson would probably emerge an easy winner. He admitted 'talking for victory', which meant that invective was his final resource in an argument, as **Oliver Goldsmith** ruefully observed:

'There's no arguing with Johnson; for when his pistol misses fire, he knocks you down with the butt end of it.'

NATIONAL LAMPOONS

What better target than the absurdities of nations and peoples?

Irish playwright **Bernard Shaw** on the maddening complacency of John Bull:

> *'The ordinary Britisher imagines that God is an Englishman.'*

The 'free-born Englishman' is a myth, according to **Bernard Shaw**:

> *'Englishmen never will be slaves; they are free to do whatever the Government and public opinion allow them to do.'*

English stolidity amused the American drama critic **Alexander Woollcott**:

> *'The English have an extraordinary ability for flying into a great calm.'*

Austin O'Malley on the impetuosity of his countrymen:

> *'An Englishman thinks seated; a Frenchman, standing; an American, pacing; an Irishman, afterwards.'*

The English can be taciturn as well as stolid. In fact, the German poet **Heinrich Heine** simply notes:

> *'Silence: a conversation with an Englishman.'*

Oscar Wilde, in his airy way, referred to

> *'One of those characteristic British faces that, once seen, are never remembered.'* — TAKE THAT!

British insularity annoys their more cosmopolitan fellow countrymen. Actor **Robert Morley**:

> *'The British tourist is always happy abroad so long as the natives are waiters.'*

The American writer **Ralph Waldo Emerson** gives this crowning example of British wrong-headedness:

> *'An English lady on the Rhine hearing a German speaking of her party as foreigners, exclaimed, "No, we are not foreigners; we are English; it is you that are foreigners." '*

Hungarian-born humorist **George Mikes'** view of the English seems unfairly dismissive:

> *'Continental people have sex life: the English have hot-water bottles.'*

A rather mild rejoinder to English insults came from the Scottish writer **John Wilson**:

> *'In all companies it gives me true pleasure to declare that, as a people, the English are very little indeed inferior to the Scotch.'*

Dr Johnson was strongly prejudiced against the Scots, and even included a sneer at their poverty in his famous dictionary:

> *'Oats. A grain which, in England is generally given to horses, but in Scotland supports the people.'*

Johnson, like many other Englishmen, resented the way in which able Scots left their own poor country to make careers across the Border. So, when a Scot defended his native land by saying it contained many 'noble wild prospects' (views), Johnson came back with

> *'Sir, the noblest prospect which a Scotchman ever sees is the high road that leads him to England!'*

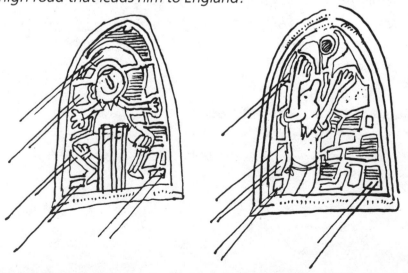

Scots were believed to be humourless, and **Sydney Smith** declared that

> *'It requires a surgical operation to get a joke well into a Scotch understanding.'*

At one time the Scots had a reputation for dubious financial transactions and insurance swindles. Hence the 19th century saying:

> *'Three failures and a fire make a Scotsman's fortune.'*

Sacrilege – a calculated insult to a British national institution from politician-businessman **Lord Mancroft**:

> *'The British have never been spiritually minded people, so they invented cricket to give them some notion of eternity.'*

Oscar Wilde was born in Ireland and made his literary career in England . . . and found neither quite satisfactory:

'If one could only teach the English how to talk and the Irish how to listen, society would be quite civilized.'

The poet **Samuel Taylor Coleridge** tries to explain away the military triumphs of the despised 'Frogs':

'Frenchmen are like grains of gunpowder – each by itself smutty and contemptible, but mass them together and they are terrible indeed.'

Sir Henry Wotton, 17th century diplomat, had a love-hate relationship with Italy, which he described as

'A paradise inhabited with devils.'

Dr Johnson exhibited one of his many national prejudices – here, inflamed by the successful American War of Independence against British rule:

'I am willing to love all mankind, except an American.'

for

'They are a race of convicts, and ought to be thankful for any thing we allow them short of hanging.'

More searchingly, **Johnson** asked:

'How is it that we hear the loudest yelps for liberty from the drivers of negroes?'

In one of his letters: **Bernard Shaw** made plain his feelings about visiting the USA:

> 'You are right in your impression that a number of persons are urging me to come to the United States. But why on earth do you call them my friends?'

Not all Americans have been fiercely patriotic. **Mark Twain** wrote:

> 'It was wonderful to find America, but it would have been more wonderful to miss it.'

Civil War leader **General Phil Sheridan** didn't love every part of the United States:

> 'If I owned Texas and Hell, I would rent out Texas and live in Hell.'

The American novelist **Henry James** settled in Europe – for good. He wrote to his sister:

> 'Dear Alice, I could come back to America (could be carried back on a stretcher) to die – but never, never to live.'

Dr Johnson's prejudices embraced the Irish as well as the Scots:

> 'The Irish are a fair people; they never speak well of one another.'

NICE ONE.

In his play *A Woman of No Importance*, **Oscar Wilde** quotes the saying, 'When good Americans die, they go to Paris.'

> LADY HUNSTANTON: *Indeed? And when bad Americans die, where do they go to?*
> LORD ILLINGWORTH: *Oh, they go to America.*

Oscar Wilde's 'defence' of the United States:

> *'It is absurd to say that there are neither ruins nor curiosities in America when they have their mothers and their manners.'*

In his playful way, **Wilde** liked to pretend that America was a skeleton in the world's cupboard:

> *'Perhaps after all America has never been discovered? I myself would merely say that it has been detected!'*

> *'Of course America had often been discovered before Columbus, but it had always been hushed up.'*

This heartfelt cry of the weaker neighbour was uttered by Mexican leader **Porfirio Diaz**:

> *'Poor Mexico, so far from God and so near to the United States!'*

Insult or ignorance? Gangster Al Capone:

> *'I don't even know what street Canada is on.'*

GOVERNMENT CUTS

Politicians trade insults among themselves, and regularly receive them from outsiders.

A character in **Bernard Shaw**'s play *Major Barbara* says of a priggish young man:

> *'He knows nothing; and he thinks he knows everything. That points clearly to a political career.'*

Sir Winston Churchill on the equipment needed by a politician:

> *'It is the ability to foretell what is going to happen tomorrow, next week, next month, and next year. And to have the ability afterwards to explain why it didn't happen.'*

Prime Minister David Lloyd George was often accused of unfair tactics, especially by supporters of the prime minister he overthrew, H. H. Asquith. Naturally, the latter's daughter, woman of letters **Margot Asquith** felt the same way about Lloyd George. She said of him:

> *'He could not see a belt without hitting below it.'*

Even in the 18th century the House of Lords was not known for its intellectual qualities. Debating whether the new peers for Westminster Bridge should be of stone or wood, **Lord Chesterfield** told the House:

> *'Of stone, to be sure, for we have too many wooden peers at Westminster already.'*

Walter Bagehot, the greatest 19th century authority on the constitution, wrote;

> *'A severe though not unfriendly critic of our institutions has said that "the cure for admiring the House of Lords was to go and look at it".'*

Lord Soper, Methodist minister and radical, on the present state of affairs:

> *'The House of Lords . . . is good evidence of life after death.'*

A character in **Oscar Wilde**'s *A Woman of No Importance* on breeding and pedigree:

> *'You should study the Peerage, Gerald . . . It is the best thing in fiction the English have ever done.'*

Only two cheers for democracy from **Bernard Shaw**:

> *'Democracy substitutes election by the incompetent many for appointment by the corrupt few.'*

A TALENT TO ABUSE

The elegant wit of the 18th century: when the Earl of Sandwich predicted that the radical **John Wilkes** would die either on the gallows or from the pox, Wilkes replied smoothly:

> *That will depend, my Lord, on whether I embrace your principles or your mistress.*

Sydney Smith was a diehard Tory. When he saw the Whig politician Lord Brougham arrive in the hall during a performance of Handel's *Messiah*, Smith remarked:

> *Here comes counsel for the other side.*

Victorian politicians tended to be a solemn lot, but **Benjamin Disraeli** was an exception. He first made himself felt by attacking the coldly correct Sir Robert Peel:

> *The Right Honourable Gentleman's smile is like the silver fittings on a coffin.*

> *The Right Honourable Gentleman is reminiscent of a poker. The only difference is that a poker gives off occasional signs of warmth.*

In the 1860s and '70s politics was dominated by the rivalry between Disraeli and Gladstone. No wonder **Disraeli**, when asked to distinguish between a misfortune and a calamity, said:

> *If Gladstone fell into the Thames, that would be a misfortune, and if anybody pulled him out, that, I suppose, would be a calamity.*

The quiet Labour leader Clement Attlee was one of **Sir Winston Churchill**'s victims:

'*He's a sheep in sheep's clothing.*'

'*Mr Attlee is a modest man. But then he has much to be modest about.*'

Quite early in his career **Sir Winston Churchill** had mastered the art of parliamentary abuse, which must be restrained but deadly:

> *'Lord Charles Beresford can best be described as one of those orators who, before they get up, do not know what they are going to say; when they are speaking, do not know what they are saying, and when they have sat down, do not know what they have said.'*

When **Churchill** wanted to attack Prime Minister Ramsay MacDonald, he told the House of Commons how he had been taken to the circus as a child but had not been allowed to see an exhibit called The Boneless Wonder . . .

> *'My parents judged that this spectacle would be too revolting and demoralizing for my youthful eyes. and I have waited fifty years to see The Boneless Wonder sitting on the Treasury Bench.'*

On another occasion **Churchill** mocked MacDonald's rather windy eloquence:

> *'We know that he has, more than any other man, the gift of compressing the largest amount of words into the smallest amount of thought.'*

One of the few men to score off Disraeli was the Radical, **John Bright**. On being told that, whatever his faults, 'Dizzy' deserved credit for being a self-made man, Bright remarked:

> *'He is a self-made man and worships his creator.'*

Labour's **Aneurin Bevan** made fun of Winston Churchill's romantic Toryism and fondness for the sound of his own voice:

'He is a man suffering from petrified adolescence.'

'He never spares himself in conversation. He gives himself so generously that hardly anybody else is permitted to give anything in his presence.'

Aneurin Bevan, a fiery Welshman, found his leaders somewhat lacking in socialist fervour. Of Clement Attlee:

'He seems determined to make a trumpet sound like a tin whistle.'

Of Hugh Gaitskell:

'A desiccated calculating machine.'

BOOM!
BOOM!

Speaking in the House of Commons **Aneurin Bevan** said he would not bother to attack the Foreign Secretary, Selwyn Lloyd, when the Prime Minister, Harold Macmillan, was present. Implying that the relationship between the two was that of servant and master, Bevan quipped:

'There is no reason to attack the monkey when the organ-grinder is present.'

In 1962 Harold Macmillan dismissed a third of his Cabinet in an attempt to save his largely discredited government. Liberal MP Jeremy Thorpe commented:

'Greater love hath no man than this, that he lay down his friends for his life.'

A TALENT TO ABUSE

The two leading Conservatives of the early 1960s, Harold Macmillan and R. A. Butler, were colleagues but not necessarily the best of friends. Labour leader **Harold Wilson** professed to believe that

> *'Every time Mr Macmillan comes back from abroad, Mr Butler goes to the airport and grips him warmly by the throat.'*

In the 1960s and '70s much was heard of Harold Wilson's poverty-stricken childhood. There were a number of sceptics, including MP **Ivor Bulwer-Thomas**:

> *'If Harold Wilson ever went to school without any boots it was merely because he was too big for them.'*

Americans have, if anything, a lower opinion of politicians than the British do. Humorist **Artemus Ward**:

> *'I'm not a politician and my other habits are good.'*

Presidential candidate **Adlai Stevenson** on the highest office:

> *'In America any boy may become President, and I suppose that's just the risk he takes.'*

Gladstone was a good man . . . but . . . according to **Disraeli**:

> *'He has not a single redeeming defect.'*

Novelist **Gore Vidal** on Ronald Reagan, the oldest man ever to become US President:

> *'A triumph of the embalmer's art.'*

Mark Twain delivers an eccentric judgement on George Washington:

> *'He was ignorant of the commonest accomplishments of youth. He could not even lie.'*

Congressman **John Randolph** of Roanoak came face to face with his enemy Henry Clay.

> CLAY: *I, sir, do not step aside for a scoundrel.*

> RANDOLPH: *On the other hand (stepping aside) I always do.*

Coolidge was known as a man who did little and said even less. When the New York wit **Dorothy Parker** was told that he had died, she asked:

> *'How can they tell?'*

Comedian **Mort Sahl**'s classic query about 'Tricky Dicky' – Richard Nixon:

> *'Would you buy a second-hand car from this man?'*

Mark Twain was sceptical about 'the American way':

'It is by the grace of God that in our country we have those three unspeakably precious things: freedom of speech, freedom of conscience, and the prudence never to practise either of them.'

Democrat **Adlai Stevenson** mocked the solemn style of his rival, General Dwight D. Eisenhower:

'The General has dedicated himself so many times, he must feel like the cornerstone of a public building.'

Thomas Dewey became Republican candidate for the presidency as a young man (by the standards of politics, anyway). Hence this comment by US Secretary of the Interior **Harold L. Ickes**:

'Dewey has thrown his diaper into the ring.'

Eisenhower's Secretary of State, Dulles, practised a belligerent 'brinkmanship' in his diplomacy. US trade union leader **Walter Reuther** called him

'Mr John Foster Dulles – the world's longest-range misguided missile.'

PROFESSIONALLY FOUL

The art of insult is perhaps most subtly practised among the learned professions. . . .

The famous advocate **F. E. Smith** often clashed with the Bench. When a judge declared that Smith's remarks had not left him much the wiser, Smith retorted:

'Not wiser, my Lord. But better informed.'

EXASPERATED JUDGE: *What do you suppose I am on the Bench for, Mr Smith?*

F. E. SMITH: *It is not for me to fathom the inscrutable ways of Providence.*

The **Reverend Sydney Smith** did not spare other men of the cloth. When a proposal was made to surround St Paul's with a wooden pavement, he suggested:

'Let the Dean and Canons lay their heads together and the thing will be done.'

Novelist **Arnold Bennett** finds a good reason for putting writers on the Honours List:

'Literature is always a good card to play for Honours. It makes people think that Cabinet ministers are educated.'

Alexander Pope's malicious portrait of the scholar:

> *The bookful blockhead, ignorantly read,*
> *With loads of learned lumber in his head.*

Army life – one of the less healthy professions, according to **H. G. Wells**:

> *'The army ages men sooner than the law and philosophy; it exposes them more freely to germs, which undermine and destroy, and it shelters them more completely from thought, which stimulates and preserves.'*

Voltaire on the physician's skills:

> *'The art of medicine consists of amusing the patient while Nature cures the disease.'*

According to **Hilaire Belloc**, in the days before the inception of the National Health Service it was only doctors who were certain to benefit from medical care:

> *They answered as they took their fees*
> *'There is no cure for this disease.'*

Liberal leader **Lord Samuel** found that the civil servant was a born obstructionist with

> *'A difficulty for every solution.'*

NICE ONE

SHOT DOWN IN FAME

The famous and the powerful have frequently borne the brunt of much witty invective. . . .

The historian Lord Macaulay maddened his contemporaries with his encyclopaedic knowledge and monopolizing of conversation:

> THOMAS CARLYLE: *Macaulay is well for a while, but one wouldn't live under Niagara.*

Jim Fiske was the most notorious of the ruthless and crooked US financiers who flourished in the 'gilded age' after the American Civil War. One anonymous wit noticed him and said:

> *'There goes Jim Fiske, with his hands in his own pockets for a change.'*

Randolph Churchill, Sir Winston's son and biographer, was a spiky character; and so was novelist **Evelyn Waugh**. When he heard that Randolph had had a non-malignant growth removed, Waugh wrote:

> *'A typical triumph of modern science to find the only part of Randolph that was not malignant — and remove it.'*

The writer Frank Harris was a powerful personality, but socially impossible. **Oscar Wilde** remarked on the result:

'Frank has been invited to every great house in England — once.'

Sir Winston Churchill on the most successful of his generals, Viscount Montgomery:

'In defeat unbeatable; in victory unbearable.'

Socialite **Margot Asquith** was introduced to film actress Jean Harlow, who irritated her by pronouncing the 't' in Margot — only to be told that

'The 't' is silent — as in Harlow.'

BOOM!
BOOM!

Kitty Muggeridge, wife of the celebrated writer and broadcaster, on the career of TV presenter David Frost:

'He rose without trace.'

Count Paul Waldersee on 'Kaiser Bill' (Wilhelm II of Germany):

'He can be most fascinating, and win hearts wherever he goes — and doesn't stay.'

SEXUAL ABUSE

The notorious 'battle of the sexes' has inspired some of the most sublime of all bitchy remarks. . . .

SAMUEL BUTLER (17th century satirical poet):

> *The souls of women are so small*
> *That some believe they've none at all.*

MADAME DE STAEL (18th century French woman of letters):

> *'The more I see of men, the more I like dogs.'*

Men have abused women so thoroughly and so often that it seems likely that they have been trying to compensate for something . . . **Max Beerbohm**:

> *'Most women are not so young as they are painted.'*

Oscar Wilde:

> *'Women give men the very gold of their lives. But they invariably want it back in small change.'*

Good old **Anonymous**:

'Women's styles may change, but their designs remain the same.'

GROAN!

Heinrich Heine:

'As soon as Eve ate the apple of wisdom, she reached for the fig-leaf; when a woman begins to think, her first thought is of a new dress.'

Anonymous strikes again:

'A youthful figure is what you get when you ask a woman her age.'

Oscar Wilde:

'One should never trust a woman who tells one her real age. A woman who would tell one that would tell one anything.'

Sometimes women have joined the chorus condemning their own sex. **Diane de Poitiers**, the French king's mistress some 450 years ago, observed that

'The years that a woman subtracts from her age are not lost. They are added to the ages of other women.'

American writer **H. L. Mencken** noted that

> 'When women kiss it always reminds me of prize-fighters shaking hands.'

Victorian novelist **George Meredith** writes with missionary assurance:

> 'I expect that Woman will be the last thing civilized by Man.'

Dr Johnson's famous put-down of a woman who did something she wasn't supposed to be capable of:

> 'Sir, a woman's preaching is like a dog's walking on his hind legs. It is not done well; but you are surprised to find it done at all.'

Women abuse men as a sex far less frequently than vice-versa. One exception was the American commentator **Helen Rowland**:

> 'The only original thing about some men is original sin.'

> 'Nowadays most women grow old gracefully; most men, disgracefully.'

One of the woman novelist **George Eliot**'s characters sums up the difference between women and men:

> 'I'm not denyin' the women are foolish: God Almighty made 'em to match the men.'

WEDDING SNAPS

The institution of marriage has taken a few hard verbal knocks in its time. . . .

Dramatist **William Congreve** on Before and After Wedlock:

'Courtship to marriage, as a very witty prologue to a very dull play.'

An anonymous male (probably a cowardly husband) claims that:

'Bigamy is having one wife too many. Monogamy is the same thing.'

Lord Chesterfield's solution to marital troubles:

'The only solid and lasting peace between a man and his wife is doubtless a separation.'

Samuel Pepys observed that misery loves company:

'Strange to say what delight we married people have to see these poor fools decoyed into our condition.'

The last word is still **St Paul**'s:

'Better marry than burn!'

Helen Rowland's view of the morning after:

'There is a vast difference beween the savage and the civilized man, but it is never apparent to their wives until after breakfast.'

POISON PENS

Writers and writings have received (and inflicted) a wide variety of criticism and contempt. . . .

The born critic can work on any material — witness the American girl who was heard to complain about the Ten Commandments:

'They don't tell you what you ought to do, and only put ideas into your head.'

A critic, **Kenneth Tynan**, on his own trade:

> *'A critic is a man who knows the way but can't drive the car.'*

The creative impotence of critics was expressed with maximum unkindness by the Irish playwright **Brendan Behan**:

> *'Critics are like eunuchs in a harem: they know how it's done, they've seen it done every day, but they're unable to do it themselves.'*

Poet laureate **Lord Tennyson** strikes down critic John Churton Collins:

> *'A louse in the locks of literature.'*

Relations between publishers and authors are often little better than those between authors and critics. A publisher's view, from **Michael Joseph**:

> *'Authors are easy enough to get on with – if you are fond of children.'*

The subtlest rebuff to an author was probably **Disraeli**'s ambiguous acknowledgement:

> *'Many thanks for your book; I shall lose no time in reading it.'*

A poet, **John Dryden**, on critics:

> *They who write ill, and they who ne'r durst write,*
> *Turn critics out of mere revenge and spite.*

Same message, but in different style, from **Groucho Marx**:

> *'From the moment I picked up your book until I laid it down I was convulsed with laughter. Some day I intend reading it.'*

As we might expect, **Dr Johnson** brought his mastery of insult to bear on contemporary literature. Asked whether Herrick or Smart was the better writer, he replied:

> *'Sir, there is no settling the precedency between a louse and a flea.'*

On one occasion **Johnson** showed his opinion of a fellow-author by complaining:

> *'Sir, I never did the man an injury; yet he would read his tragedy to me.'*

Dorothy Parker on a work of fiction:

> *'This is not a novel to be tossed aside lightly. It should be thrown with great force.'*

TAKE THAT!

A. A. Milne's whimsical stories about Winnie the Pooh and Christopher Robin did not appeal to **Dorothy Parker**. Reviewing *The House at Pooh Corner* in her 'Constant Reader' column, she came to a point in the book at which:

> *'Tonstant Weader fwowed up.'*

Reviewing A. A. Milne's play *Give Me Yesterday*, **Dorothy Parker** wrote sarcastically:

> *'Its hero is caused, by a novel device, to fall asleep and a-dream; and thus he is given yesterday. Me, I should have given him twenty years to life.'*

One of the books **Dorothy Parker** most disliked was *The Autobiography of Margot Asquith*. The tone of the autobiography can be gathered from **Dorothy Parker**'s comment that

> *'The affair between Margot Asquith and Margot Asquith will live as one of the prettiest love stories in all literature.'*

Parker defined an optimist as

> *'One who thought that Margot Asquith wasn't going to write any more.'*

Complaints about obscurity in literature are not new. **King James I** said of the poet John Donne:

> *'Dr Donne's verses are like the peace of God; they pass all understanding.'*

In speaking, a pause makes all the difference. When the poet Southey fished for compliments to his epic *Madoc*, the classical scholar **Richard Porson** told him:

> *'Madoc will be remembered . . . when Homer and Virgil are forgotten.'*

While **Charles Dickens** was editing a magazine, a young poet submitted 'Orient Pearls at Random Strung' to him.
   The novelist returned it with the comment:

'Too much string.'

Oscar Wilde on the pugnacious versifier W. E. Henley:

'He has fought a good fight and has had to face every difficulty except – popularity.'

Of a famous Victorian tear-jerker, Dickens's *Old Curiosity Shop*, **Oscar Wilde** remarked:

'One must have a heart of stone to read the death of little Nell without laughing.'

Oscar Wilde swats a novelist and a poet with a single blow:

'Meredith is a prose Browning, and so is Browning.'

Oscar Wilde's opinion of a ponderously portentous contemporary:

'Henry James writes fiction as if it were a painful duty.'

Novelist **Virginia Woolf** was not impressed when she read James Joyce's once-shocking *Ulysses*, dismissing it as

'The work of a queasy undergraduate scratching his pimples.'

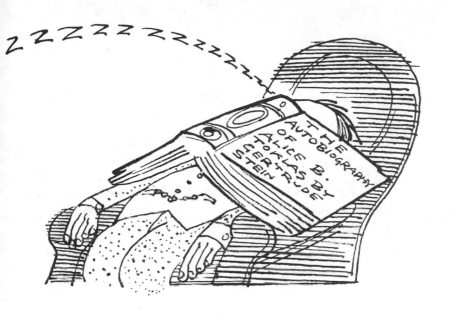

The American critic **Clifton Fadiman** on the experimental writing of Gertrude Stein:

'Miss Stein was a past master in making nothing happen very slowly.'

When Gertrude Stein published *Everybody's Autobiography*, **Fadiman** wrote that

'I found nothing really wrong with this autobiography except poor choice of subject.'

The poet **Philip Larkin** says of modern novels:

'Many have a beginning, a muddle, and an end.'

A TALENT TO ABUSE

Logan Pearsall Smith on the rewards and punishments of popular fiction:

> 'A best-seller is the gilded tomb of a mediocre talent.'

American drama critic **Eugene Field** gave this classic verdict on an actor's nervous and understated performance as King Lear:

> 'Mr Clark played the King as though somebody else might be about to play the Ace.'

NICE ONE

A characteristic shaft from well-known New York critic **Walter Kerr**:

> 'Hook and Ladder *is the sort of play that gives failures a bad name.*'

The *Punch* writer **Douglas Jerrold**, when told that the actor Henry Holl had left the stage and set up as a wine merchant, commented:

> 'Oh yes, and I'm told that his wine off the stage is better than his whine on it.'

Irish dramatist Bernard Shaw dominated — and irritated — several generations with his talents . . . which included a gift for self-advertisement. The writer **'Saki'** satirized Shaw as

> 'Sherard Blaw, the dramatist who had discovered himself, and who had given so ungrudgingly of his discovery to the world.'

Israel Zangwill on Shaw:

'The way Bernard Shaw believes in himself is very refreshing in these atheistic days when so many people believe in no God at all.'

Bernard Shaw combined universal benevolence with insufferable conceit. The result, according to **Oscar Wilde**, was that

'He hasn't an enemy in the world, and none of his friends like him.'

The playwright **Henry Arthur Jones** developed an obsessive hatred of Bernard Shaw, whom he described as a b-----, or at any rate

'A freakish homunculus germinated outside lawful procreation.'

After the first night of one of **Oscar Wilde**'s plays, an ill-wisher handed him – a cabbage. Unruffled, Wilde sniffed it appreciatively and said:

'Thank you, my dear fellow. Every time I smell it, I shall be reminded of you.'

Writer **Rose Macaulay** describes a piece of over-light entertainment:

'It was a book to kill time for those who like it better dead.'

MOVIE MOCKERY

The moguls and stars of the film business have refined the snide retort to a fine art. . . .

Even in the palmiest days of Hollywood, writers were not treated with much respect by the big producers. The famous novelist **Scott Fitzgerald** noted:

> *'You always knew where you stood with Sam Goldwyn: nowhere.'*

Screenwriter **Herman Mankiewicz** had a poor opinion of screen-writers:

> *'I know lots of $75 a week writers, but they're all making $1,500 a week.'*

The producer knows best: Hungarian-born **Joe Pasternak**:

> *'You call this a script? Give me a couple of $5,000 a week writers and I'll write it myself.'*

A TALENT TO ABUSE

Irish writer **St John Ervine**:

> *'American motion pictures are written by the half-educated for the half-witted.'*

Humorist **Will Rogers** had much the same opinion:

> *'There is only one thing that can kill the movies; and that is education.'*

Louis Sherwin on Hollywood standards:

> *'They know only one word of more than one syllable here, and that is* fillum.'
>
> GROAN!

Columnist **Walter Winchell** called Hollywood

> *'A place where they shoot too many pictures and not enough actors.'*

Curiously enough, one of the greatest American directors, **D. W. Griffith,** was scornful of Hollywood's pretensions:

> *'The Academy of Motion Picture Arts and Sciences? What art? What science?'*

Hollywood gossip columnist **Hedda Hopper** went to the cinema and

'For the first time in my life I envied my feet. They were asleep.'

Hollywood's men of power were not popular. **Herman Mankiewicz** on Louis B. Mayer:

'There, but for the grace of God, goes God.'

French writer and film director **Jean Cocteau** on a technical advance pioneered by Hollywood in the belief that 'Big is Beautiful':

'CinemaScope? The next time I write a poem I shall use a larger piece of paper.'

Harry Cohn was the legendarily unpleasant and colossally unpopular head of Colombia Pictures. Observing the throng at his funeral, actor **Red Skelton** remarked:

'It proves what they always say: give the public what they want, and they'll come out for it.'

Sid Grauman:

'I saw this empty taxicab drive up, and out stepped Sam Goldwyn.'

Film director **Billy Wilder** welcomed the arrival of television:

> *'I'm delighted with it, because it used to be that films were the lowest form of art. Now we've got something to look down on.'*

Sam Goldwyn explained why there were crowds at Louis B. Mayer's funeral:

> *'The only reason so many people showed up was to make sure he was dead.'*

ART ATTACKS

The creative fraternity are often the target of cruel and sarcastic wit. . . .

Basic music criticism from **Dr Johnson,** after hearing a violinist:

'Difficult do you call it, Sir? I wish it were impossible.'

Ludwig van Beethoven to a fellow-composer:

'I liked your opera. I think I will set it to music.'

Rossini's opinion of a younger competitor:

'Monsieur Wagner has lovely moments but some terrible quarters-of-an-hour.'

Oscar Wilde had nothing (well, almost nothing) but praise for the Teutonic thunder of Wagner's operas:

'I like Wagner's music better than any other music. It is so loud that one can talk the whole time without people hearing what one says. That is a great advantage.'

Mark Twain proffered a back-handed compliment to the German genius:

> *'Wagner's music is better than it sounds.'*

Hollywood columnist **Hedda Hopper** reviews:

> *'Her singing was mutiny on the High Cs.'*

Orson Welles's opinion of teenybopper idol Donny Osmond:

> *'He has Van Gogh's ear for music.'* — *TAKE THAT!*

Oscar Levant on the kidnapping of Frank Sinatra Jr:

> *'It must have been done by music critics.'*

Nancy Banks Smith voices a widely held view of 'modernism' and 'post-modernism':

> *'If you have to keep the lavatory door shut by extending your left leg, it's modern architecture.'*

Two cracks at the man with the camera, by American novelist **Gore Vidal**:

> *'Photography is the "art form" of the untalented.'*
>
> *'One word is worth a thousand pictures.'*

Albert Wolff, an influential critic who attacked the Impressionist painters, was also a singularly ugly man. Degas dismissed Wolff's comments, saying:

'How could he understand? He came to Paris by way of the trees.'

When the art critic **John Ruskin** dared to attack the painter James McNeill Whistler he was sued. Yet all Ruskin said was:

'I have seen, and heard, much of cockney impudence before now; but never expected to hear a coxcomb ask two hundred guineas for flinging a pot of paint in the public's face.'

As a young man, Oscar Wilde regarded himself as **Whistler**'s disciple. When Whistler coined a particularly brilliant epigram, Wilde sighed 'I wish I'd said that!'

'You will, Oscar. You will.'